Understanding Young Children's Learning through Play

This timely and accessible text introduces, theorises and practically applies two important concepts which now underpin early years practice, those of 'playful learning' and 'playful pedagogies'. Pat Broadhead and Andy Burt draw upon filmed material, conversations with children, reflection, observation, and parental and staff interviews, in their longitudinal study of outdoor and indoor play environments in an early years unit. This research-based text offers extensive insights into related theories as well as drawing on their skills and knowledge, as researcher and as class teacher, to provide opportunities for personal reflection and possibilities for practical application in early years classes and settings.

Discussing both indoor and outdoor environments, the text explores ideas around 'open-ended play', and 'the whatever you want it to be place'. It illustrates how the themes of children's play reflect their interests, experiences, knowledge gained at home and in school and their cultural heritages. By showing how children become familiar and skilful within open-ended play environments, the authors illustrate how the children's cooperative skills develop over time as they become connected communities of learners. Alongside the examples of children's playful learning, the book also considers the implications for resourcing and organising playful settings through playful pedagogies that can connect with the Early Years Foundation Stage curriculum (DfES 2007) and with the Tickell Review, ongoing as the book went to press.

The book incorporates children's perspectives on their play to illustrate how rich their personal understandings are. It also includes parental reflections on what may initially appear a risky and unusual outdoor environment, and it draws attention to the importance of conflict resolution in play to extend children's resilience and assertiveness.

This insightful text will be of interest to students of early years education, early years practitioners, academics and researchers.

Pat Broadhead is Professor of Playful Learning at Leeds Metropolitan University.

Andy Burt was the Early Years Coordinator at Fishergate Primary School during the joint research and is now the deputy head teacher at Bishopthorpe Infant School in York.

Understanding Young Children's Learning through Play

Building playful pedagogies

Pat Broadhead and Andy Burt

Routledge
Taylor & Francis Group
LONDON AND NEW YORK

First published 2012
by Routledge
2 Park Square, Milton Park, Abingdon, Oxon OX14 4RN

Simultaneously published in the USA and Canada
by Routledge
711 Third Avenue, New York, NY 10017

Routledge is an imprint of the Taylor & Francis Group, an informa business

British Library Cataloguing in Publication Data
A catalogue record for this book is available from the British Library

Library of Congress Cataloging in Publication Data
Broadhead, Pat, 1951-
Understanding young children's learning through play : building playful
pedagogies / Pat Broadhead, Andy Burt.
p. cm.
Includes bibliographical references and index.
1. Play. 2. Early childhood education. 3. Early childhood education—
Parent participation. I. Burt, Andy. II. Title.
LB1137.B764 2012
372.21–dc23
2011021490

ISBN: 978–0–415–61427–6 (hbk)
ISBN: 978–0–415–61428–3 (pbk)
ISBN: 978–0–203–15634–6 (ebk)

Typeset in Bembo by Prepress Projects Ltd, Perth, UK

MIX
Paper from
responsible sources
FSC
www.fsc.org   FSC® C004839

Printed and bound in Great Britain by
TJ International Ltd, Padstow, Cornwall

To the wonderfully creative children and staff of
Fishergate Primary School

Contents

Figures

Tables

Acknowledgements

We would like to thank Andy Herbert, head teacher at Fishergate Primary School, for allowing this research to be undertaken. We would also like to thank the children, parents and the early years team without whom it could not have happened. Especial thanks to the parents for permission to reproduce the children's pictures. The children's names and those of the early years team members have been changed for anonymity.

Introduction

The book has arisen from a longitudinal study of children's play over several months in the early years unit at Fishergate School in York. The children are aged from three to five years, bringing together nursery- and reception-aged children with an early years team of educators. The two joint researchers brought their respective skills and knowledge to the study of this play environment. Pat Broadhead brought her own long-standing interests and experience in observing and researching playful learning in the early years, and her knowledge of the theoretical frameworks that assist our understanding of the complexities of playful learning and playful pedagogies. Andy Burt, as the teacher in charge of the unit during the period of research, brought a deep interest in the development of open-ended play experiences for children, good knowledge of the children as players and learners, including their home backgrounds, a dedication to enriching the play experiences of the children through pedagogical developments, and excellent relationships with the early years team that also encouraged their participation in the research. Together we were all able to address theory–practice links in a wide range of ways, using filmed material, observation, reflective conversations and semi-structured interviews.

The longitudinal element has enabled the authors to address that elusive concept of learning and progression though play across a community of learners (children and adults) in a systematic and combined study of insider and outsider perspectives and in so doing, to track the development of knowledge and understanding for children, through playful learning, in an educational setting. The research has also been able to consider in depth the continuity of learning and experience across the key years, ages three, four and five, and to look at the ways in which pedagogical decisions and provision can deepen the impact of continuous, stimulating provision. We are looking especially in this study at the provision of open-ended play materials and the forthcoming chapters are an in-depth exploration of this form of pedagogical provision.

The book presents a model which is explored and unpacked as the chapters unfold. The model juxtaposes playful pedagogy through the study of 'open-ended play' with playful learning as 'the whatever you want it to be place' as in Table 0.1. The subsequent chapters explain how the juxtaposition might help

Table 0.1 Playful pedagogies and playful learning: the juxtaposition model

'Open-ended play': understanding playful pedagogies	'The whatever you want it to be place': revealing playful learning
A way for the adult to conceive of her/ his own role in creating and sustaining an educational environment that is flexible enough to allow children's interests and experiences to emerge and develop; it also encompasses the adults' responsibilities in identifying, recording and planning for those interests in systematic but flexible ways and a responsibility to look for ways of extending those interests and relating them to the wider world in which the child is living and learning. The early years setting becomes a space and place where adults nurture potential and push the boundaries of their personal understandings of playful learning and playful pedagogies.	The environment and its possibilities as perceived and engaged with from the child's perspective. The child enters a space where anything is possible – whether a large or small space – and where they can engage alone or with others in exploring and exploiting that environment to match the images, plans and memories that emerge from their own minds, experiences and skills. The early years setting becomes a space and place where children explore their identity, potential and interests and push back the boundaries of personal possibility through playful engagement.

practitioners to think about and plan for optimum ways of supporting children's learning through play in an early years educational setting. At Fishergate early years unit, the early years team have, over time, provided resources and spaces for children that include a wide range of open-ended materials both outdoors and indoors. However, they still deliver the curriculum requirements and indeed were pleased to exploit the playful aspects of the Early Years Foundation Stage (EYFS) when it was introduced in 2007 (DfES 2007).

Perhaps what the book and practices at Fishergate do most substantially is to show how child-initiated and child-directed play can lead the day-to-day experiences of the children whilst still accommodating teacher-initiated pedagogical strategies and, on a day-to-day basis, also including teacher-directed activities linked to the formal teaching of literacy and numeracy. We also see informal instances of children's engagements with both literacy and numeracy through their self-directed play activities but the purpose of these activities is never to provide 'sites' for literacy and numeracy; it is just that children use what they know when they need to use it. The early years team have worked out a way to balance these requirements whilst still allowing much of the day to be given over to playful engagements led by children's interests, experiences, memories and cultural frames of reference drawn from their home and community cultures. The book aims to capture their practical approaches alongside detailed, interpreted vignettes that show children's playful and, on many occasions, highly interactive engagements in the open-ended play environment.

What the book also aims to show is that there is very little *pretence* in children's play; these children draw from life experiences which arise from many sources and re-engage with them through play as a way of seeking to actively understand the world around them and their own place within that complex world. Those experiences may come from home, the media, the community or school itself but they are all part of becoming who they are as individuals, and the book is also about identity and play. Also, much of what children do is often described as 'repetition', and this book would also want to challenge this as too narrow a construct in relation to interpreting or understanding children's play; rather, it intends to show how what children do is to conduct the same experiment many times but often under slightly different conditions. To *pretend* is to be something other than who you are but our joint research suggests that when children play they are wholly themselves because they are fully absorbed and unremittingly committed to their activities.

Chapter 1 introduces the school and the early years team and explains how the research came about. The methodology for the study is explained, including the ethics of researching with children and the importance of hearing their voices when exploring their play decisions and activities. The chapter also considers why there has been such variability in the status of play in English early years policy and looks at some of the underpinning and changing theoretical perspectives which frame our understanding of playful learning and the development of playful pedagogies.

Chapter 2 introduces the outdoor area at Fishergate, where the journey towards open-ended playful pedagogies really began to 'take off' for the early years team. Throughout the book, we hear reflective perspectives from all the early years team members; these highlight and illuminate the inter-connections between 'thinking' and 'doing' when changes are occurring in practice and provision. The capacity and willingness of all the team members to be reflective is a significant part of making changing practices effective in relation to enhancing children's learning. Chapter 2 introduces the reader to the first three of 15 play vignettes in the book. These three vignettes are extended accounts of children's play as captured on film and, whenever possible, shown to the children for their reflections, and in many cases also watched several times by Andy and Pat for reflective interpretation and meaning-making in coming to understand the impact of open-ended play provision on children's playful learning. Throughout the book, the vignettes are linked to the EYFS to illustrate the potential for open-ended play for curriculum delivery through child-initiated activity and play.

Chapter 3 links playful learning with children's cultural experiences and with the development of identity. It examines open-ended play in the outdoors and also considers changes and developments in indoor provision at Fishergate early years unit. The chapter considers the extent to which family life influences play and becomes integral to progression in play in educational settings. It also considers how children's developing understanding of neighbourhood and community also influences their play when open-ended resources are available to them for extended periods of time. Chapter 3 focuses also on the importance of nurturing friendships and how this is linked to identity development for young children and expressed through play in an early years setting. Identity develops from engagement with others and the early years are important times for developing a strong sense of self as appropriately active and interactive within a wider community.

Chapter 4 focuses on the role of and challenges for the adult when working in an open-ended play environment in an educational setting. We argue that current policy often militates against the liberation of adults to be creative, flexible, reflective pedagogues, especially within the context of Foundation Stage assessments, which have, for a long time, been outcomes driven and extensive at the end of the Foundation Stage. It details the daily activity at Fishergate in terms of child-initiated and adult-initiated activities and also illustrates the ways in which adults have changed practice in order to work and play alongside the children in taking the children's interests as starting points for co-constructed playful learning. Chapter 4 addresses the pedagogical dilemma of deciding whether or not to intervene in children's play – when is scaffolding appropriate and helpful to children and what form should it take? It looks at how a student teacher is supported in understanding her role within an environment where child-initiated activity takes precedence, and vignettes are included to illustrate this aspect. This chapter also offers some extended reflective commentaries from children which show how well they understand the processes at work as they play.

Chapter 4 considers gender as a pedagogical feature drawing on vignettes already developed in the book and examining related policy and literature. Although boys and girls do play as single gender groups at Fishergate, there are several play events that show how boys and girls and older and younger children are attracted to integrated play experiences with open-ended resources with which they are familiar.

Chapter 5 examines risk, including the risks that children take and meet in this play environment and the risks that adults take in developing what may initially look like rather unconventional play activities and environments in an early years educational setting. The early years team have already reflected in previous chapters on why they work as they do – because the quality of the children's play is so much greater than anything they were seeing in the days before they worked in this way. The chapter also focuses through vignettes on conflict and conflict resolution. Risk-taking and conflict resolution are paired in this way because each of these aspects can be a source of anxiety for educators and yet they are both very important aspects of identity development and cultural assimilation at any stage of life.

Chapter 6 looks at the longitudinal development of four children, captured on film across the months of filming. It aims to illustrate their progress from new child to expert player in these 'whatever you want them to be' spaces and places. We look also at how new children have to learn to 'map' the indoor and outdoor spaces before they can make the journey towards expert player status. We illustrate how, when left to their own play themes and interests in the right kind of environment, the things that children choose to do are often more complex, challenging and satisfying than anything an adult might suggest to them or lead them into.

Chapter 7 is the concluding chapter. It is presented in three parts. Part one draws together findings from the study of the whatever you want it to be place and on what children's playful learning has revealed from children's perspectives and in terms of children's playful progression. Part two focuses on drawing together understandings of playful pedagogies in open-ended play environments and what we have learned about changing practice on this development journey for educators. Part three looks at the complicated business of bringing balance to an early years environment in terms of child-initiated and teacher-initiated activities. This final section also attempts to read the runes for the future as the Tickell recommendations for the revisions to the EYFS have recently been published.

The book aims to reveal in some detail the description of the play environment at Fishergate early years unit. It was an exciting place in which to study playful learning because so much of interest was happening on a daily basis. However, we are not suggesting that every early years educational setting should look like this one in order to have the best chance of nurturing playful learning and playful progression. We have also tried to show how the moves towards the development of this playful learning environment were gradual and were supported by team-based discussions and decision-making. We hope the book can support early years educators and also primary school educators in thinking about how their educational environments support thinking, learning and decision-making by children and by adults together, as communities of playful learners.

Chapter 1

The background to the book

The school, the research and recent developments in policy and theory

This study draws from a year in the life of the early years unit at Fishergate Primary School in York, England. The unit serves children aged from three years until the end of their reception year. Andy Burt, one of the book's authors, was the teacher in charge of the unit until July 2011 and, with the early years team, had been developing approaches to open-ended play in the unit for several years – we will explain what we mean by 'open-ended play' as the book unfolds, as we try to illustrate the concept as an holistic approach to teaching and learning in the early years and also explain how it links with the implementation of the Early Years Foundation Stage and the day-to-day responsibilities of practitioners in early years settings.

This book aims to support early years practitioners in deepening their understanding of what 'playful learning' might mean and look like and what 'playful pedagogies' are and might do in their classroom or early years setting. This focus on learning requires a focus on children's playful activities, and the joint research undertaken by Andy and Pat has looked closely at children's play in an open-ended, school-based play environment over a period of several months. Pedagogy is what adults do to provide learning and teaching experiences, but pedagogy is also informed by an educator's own understanding about why they do what they do. Consequently, it is necessary to talk to and research with the adults in the early years setting to try and capture these pedagogical insights around playful learning, and our joint research has aimed to do this. This research underpinning this book has been designed to try and capture each of these complex aspects – learning and teaching – and to try and better understand the relationship between them through better understanding the day-to-day business of playful learning in an early years unit.

This book aims to capture the impact of these developments on the children, on the team members and, where possible, more broadly across the school and in relation to parents and carers. Pat Broadhead has been researching open-ended play and its links with the growth of sociability and cooperation for several years (Broadhead 2004, 2006, 2010; Broadhead *et al.* 2010). She has observed children becoming increasingly expert at playing together as they become more familiar with one another and with the materials and resources available to them. She has also studied the connections between cooperative play and intellectual challenge for young children in relation to traditional play materials including sand, water, large and small construction and role play, and in relation to open-ended play materials that are sufficiently flexible to allow children to create their own play themes around the materials. Where intellectual challenge is in evidence amongst groups or pairs of interacting peers, learning-in-action is also most likely to be evident; however, intellectual challenge and learning potential are not necessarily easily recognised when children are playing; they have to be searched for. The study of children's playful engagements in their early years settings is relatively recent but increasing numbers of studies are becoming available (Brock 1999; Howard 2010; Martlew *et al.* 2011; Nutbrown 2006; Rogers and Evans 2008; Worthington 2010a). However, there continues to be debate and contention in this complex area (Wood 1997).

Two of the biggest challenges for both practitioners and researchers are, first, to understand how play in an early years educational setting is linked with learning for the playing children and, second, to share this understanding with those with whom they work but also with those who are more sceptical about the benefits of play as self-initiated intellectual pursuit and as a way of understanding ourselves and our interests as we gradually make meaning in the complex world around us. We hope to bring some of these complexities to life in the following chapters.

Meeting and engaging in joint research

Andy and Pat first met several years ago when Andy was the Year 1 teacher in another York school. At that time, Pat had been researching play with the reception teacher in the school and with other reception teachers in York schools on a project funded by City of York Local Education Authority and York University (Broadhead 2004). We had been researching the levels of sociability and cooperation that children were showing as they played together with a range of traditionally available play materials (sand, water, large construction, small construction and small world and role play). We used an observational schedule, the Social Play Continuum (SPC) (Broadhead 2004, 2006). This requires the observer to record specified, observed characteristics of play. These characteristics are organised into four domains showing increasing complexity and intellectual challenge in the play: the Associative Domain, the Social Domain, the Highly Social Domain and the Cooperative Domain. As well as recording the play in this quantitative way, we made extensive notes of qualitative descriptions of the play and also undertook joint discussion after we had completed our quantitative-qualitative observations of play. To our surprise, during the joint research, the use of the SPC revealed that the role play stimulated the lowest levels of cooperative play. The Cooperative Domain, as defined and described on the SPC, has the highest levels of intellectual challenge and a very small number of role play observations were categorised as being located in the Cooperative Domain.

When discussing this at a project meeting in this earlier project, one reception teacher had suggested that it might be because the role play areas were themed by adults, as a home corner (in two reception classes), a shop, a café and a party, but the other areas we had been observing, especially the sand, water and large construction, were non-thematic; they were in effect much more open-ended. As a result, we had seen from our observations that children introduced and developed their own play themes in these areas and became more absorbed and more committed to them than they were to the role play; it was these high levels of commitment that brought the play into the Cooperative Domain with its associated high levels of intellectual challenge.

Leading on from this, we introduced what we called *open-ended role play areas* in the five classes, using cardboard boxes, cardboard tubes, cable reels, fabrics, old wooden clothes horses and other materials. Further joint observations undertaken by the researcher and the teacher in this new area had revealed that the play moved rapidly into the Cooperative Domain (as measured on the Social Play Continuum). In one of the classrooms, the teacher, in discussion with the children, said she was 'tired of calling it the open-ended role play area'; it was such a mouthful. One girl said it could be called 'the whatever you want it to be place' (Broadhead 2004: 73). In saying this, she was acknowledging that this open-ended area enabled the children to determine and develop the play themes – unlike the themed areas that adults had provided in the previous research such as the shop or the party. Much of Pat's subsequent research has focussed on developing these ideas in conjunction with a range of early years practitioners.

However, during this earlier project, Andy had seen the joint research ongoing in the reception class of the school in which he was then working. He wanted to introduce the ideas into his Year 1 classroom and so we began to work together with the Year 1 children introducing open-ended play materials into the classroom.

One thing Pat noticed was that Andy seemed prepared to give the children high levels of freedom, at an early stage, with the new open-ended play materials; sometimes the play appeared noisy and chaotic but the use of the SPC observational schedule showed that the play was cooperative and full of problem-setting and solving, rich uses of language and joint goal-setting and achievement. To an untrained eye, however, this richness might have seemed lost in the apparent chaos. As a researcher, Pat had undertaken many observations of play in a wide range of settings but it emerged that the combination of an open-ended play space along with an early years teacher willing to let this unfamiliar space be taken over by the children to quite a considerable extent led to some exciting and highly engaged play as we researched together in the Year 1 classroom.

The joint research came to an end and the link between Andy and Pat was lost for a range of reasons. It was several years later that Andy emailed Pat, who was working at Leeds Metropolitan University, to ask if she wanted to come and look at some of the ways in which he had developed the ideas over the years. This book is the result of subsequent work between the staff team in the Fishergate early years unit and a play researcher.

Introducing the school and the team

Fishergate School is in a Victorian, two-story building close to the city centre of York. There are just over 200 children in the school and, on average, around 45 children per morning and afternoon session in the early years unit. These are 30 reception-aged children and 15 nursery children from the age of three years. The school serves a mixed and very broad catchment with children from privately owned houses, a large number living in council houses and flats and some in privately rented accommodation. Some children live in sheltered housing as a result of domestic violence in the family. Children also regularly attend from a local, permanent traveller's site. Children have occasionally attended who live in houseboats on the river. There are regular attenders with a parent in the armed services and children with a parent or parents attending the University of York. The population of the school overall is quite transient, with children leaving before Year 6 on a regular basis. Within the early years unit, the children's lifestyles outside school have some very marked contrasts, with some living in relative affluence and others in poverty with all its attendant challenges. There are always some children in the unit with the potential for challenging behaviour resulting from the difficulties and lifestyles being experienced by children, parents or both in the home and wider community. In addition, there were some children with statements of special need and children in the process of assessment for a statement within the unit during the period of research.

When Andy was appointed to the post in 2005, the numbers of children in the unit were quite low with spare capacity available. From 2007, the numbers of pupils began to increase with a full reception intake since 2007 and a full nursery intake since 2009. This increase in numbers may have resulted from the good Ofsted (Office for Standards in Education, Children's Services and Skills) report of 2006 but, as the next chapter also shows, it also coincides with the developments and significant changes in the outdoor play area. The staff team have also noted that an increasing number of parents are coming to look around because they have been told about the unit and how it works by other parents; this may have impacted on the increase in pupil numbers and may also be linked to the gradual introduction of a more open-ended approach to teaching and learning through the expansion of flexible play resources and materials.

The outdoor area is described in more detail in the next chapter, with developments to the indoor areas, which followed the focus on the outdoors, being described in Chapter 3.

The early years team

Andy has been the early years leader in the unit since 2005. Prior to this he worked for six years in another school in York, in Year 1 and in the reception class, having qualified in 1999. He has been an Advanced Skills Teacher since 2008, taking one day a week supporting other schools and settings. Over the last two years, there have been increasing requests from within and beyond the Local Authority for Andy to talk about the developing approaches to playful learning and teaching in the early years unit, and along with this, regular visitors to the unit. He became deputy head at another York school in September 2011, a school that was taking creativity and exploration into the Key Stage (KS) 1 and KS2.

The subsequent staff descriptions begin with self-selected pseudonyms.

Debbie had left school knowing she wanted to work in childcare. She had worked for several years in a private nursery 'moving up through the ranks, from assistant, to senior, to deputy manager'. Having been there a while and because of personal circumstances, she felt it was time for a change. She saw a post advertised in a local school, applied and was unsuccessful at interview but then applied at Fishergate, was interviewed and was accepted. Although the work represented a drop in salary she decided to accept the job. Debbie is responsible for the general set-up of the unit, 'meeting and greeting parents' and working with the children in a general way with no specific responsibilities for individual children other than her key worker group for which all staff have responsibility. In deciding where to go to engage with children she would 'scan the room and mooch around but try not to make my presence known or interrupt them'.

Elizabeth had qualified with an NNEB (National Nursery Examination Board qualification) and begun working on a paediatric ward in a local hospital, working there for 15 years with children from birth to 15 years of age. She had taken further training to develop her knowledge of hospital play. When she had her own children, the shift work was difficult to continue. She then took part-time work in a local supermarket and gradually built up supply work in a number of early years settings. She had undertaken supply work at Fishergate and was then asked by Andy if she would provide full-time cover for a member of staff who was leaving. Although temporary in the first instance, Elizabeth had been at Fishergate full-time for four years. Her role is general with some administrative responsibilities and she occasionally took responsibility for children with special educational needs.

Jane had begun working with a mixed Year 1/2 class at Fishergate. Towards the end of the research period, Jane had moved into the early years unit to support two children with special educational needs and at the time of the research was working full-time, engaged with the two children for the majority of the time but also working and playing with others on occasion. She had worked as a teaching assistant elsewhere in York and Yorkshire and had begun her working life as a hairdresser. She had also worked in banking, retail and administration but decided that she 'wanted to do something worthwhile that she could enjoy and help others with'.

Rachel had worked as a parent volunteer at Fishergate employed one day a week although this was to rise to three days during the research period. She, her husband and her children had travelled for two years in Bangladesh and on returning found that the children could not be accepted back into their previous primary school. Rachel had visited Fishergate and felt it was 'unique' and 'a very inclusive school with a welcoming ethos'. She was also completing a part-time BA in Early Years and felt she was able to put the ideas about play that she was engaging with into practice, as well as to better understand the meaning of 'following the child's interests' at Fishergate. Over the period of her involvement with Fishergate, Rachel felt she had seen a substantial change in practice evolve since Andy's arrival.

Vicky began working in the unit as the joint research was drawing to a close. Previously she had worked as a teaching assistant supporting a child with Down's syndrome. She then undertook a psychology degree, had three children of her own and trained as a breast-feeding counsellor, working for a local Sure Start programme. She had also undertaken other counselling work with parents on Sure Start projects. Her role at Fishergate was as a general team member. She had been temporarily employed to cover a substantial intake of children to the unit in the previous January.

Thus, although staff numbers may seem generous overall, it should be recalled that some of the staff were temporary and some were part-time and, at the time of the staff semi-structured interviews, the pupil numbers were at their highest, thus requiring an increased pupil–staff ratio.

The research unfolds: methods, challenges and ethical practices

The substantive period of data collection for the research began early in 2009 and continued until just before Easter in 2010. This allowed longitudinal data collection of the expert players aged five years who had been in the unit since age three along with new entrants and the progressing four-year-olds. Social life is notoriously difficult to research (and classrooms are sites of social engagement). Social life has an 'emergent quality' to it and there are influences upon it to cause it to change over time; as a consequence the descriptions change also as they are subject to this substantial range of influences (Scott and Morrison 2006: 164). Play is a form of social engagement and so also subject to changes in its expressions, making it difficult to research out of its wider contexts and difficult to convey its complexities in standardised ways. In seeking to study the play over time, we hoped to bring some measure of authenticity to the research. A key part of understanding the influences upon playful learning and the development of playful pedagogies was therefore the reflexive discussions that Andy and Pat undertook in watching the filmed material. We needed to build a shared understanding of what we were seeing from our respective perspectives as insider and outsider and it was obvious that this would take time. Gergen and Gergen (2003: 579) identify the pitfalls of *reflexivity* as research method when they say:

Here, investigators seek ways of demonstrating to their audiences their historical and geographical situatedness, their personal investments in the research, various biases they bring to their work, their surprises and 'undoings' in the process of their research endevor (*sic*).

By working together we offer some degree of check and balance on play interpretations and this was also why we tried to watch the play episodes as often as time would allow. By also capturing some children's play over time, we also had some comparative material for deepening reflection and understanding of what was happening when children played.

There was no funding for this research; it arose from a desire to try and better understand the play and its impact. Pat made 13 visits to the unit over this period and Andy and Pat also met during school holiday periods to reflect on the material as and when they each had time available from their other responsibilities. Pat also made visits for interviews and conversations with the wider staff team.

The main research method was to film the children's play, quite randomly, either indoors or outdoors and to use this as a subsequent basis for discussion with the children involved and with the early years team, although it was most substantially Andy and Pat who watched and reflected on the films as noted above. These conversations have been central to the development of the ideas being shared in this book as together, and over time, we tried to unpick what it was that the children were learning by trying to get a stronger sense of the continuity and development within the play. The play episodes have been viewed by Andy and Pat and discussed many times. In reflecting on the children's play in the reflexive ways described above, we hoped that a deep immersion over time would bring levels of understanding to better support the eventual analysis and dissemination of the data.

In working together, we brought together insider and outsider perspectives. Andy knew the children, their families and their prior and daily experiences in depth and was also leading on the pedagogical developments arising from his personal interests in the potential of open-ended play. Pat brought broad theoretical frameworks around play scholarship as well as experience as a play researcher and observer and a particular research-based interest in the implementation of open-ended approaches and their potential for positive impact on children's learning. More information was needed on how such influences worked and how they might be captured.

Whilst gathering the filmed data, Pat might cease filming to have a conversation with a team member about the play as they recounted related episodes over periods when Pat had not been present. Pat would then record these conversations quickly in her journal and then continue filming; consequently there might be breaks in some play episodes. Some play episodes might be filmed for an hour or so, others might be briefer. Sometimes, in the background of a film clip, we would see incidental activity (that is, incidental to the current filming focus) that we would note was a continuation of something seen perhaps the previous week. There was no attempt to be systematic in the filming, which would have been impossible with so many children in the unit and so little time to film. The main driver was to look around, see what was happening and start to film based on the premise that there would always be something of interest and value in the children's play activities.

Pat also tried to keep a balance between filming indoor and outdoor activities at each filming session and between boys and girls, who sometimes played as single-gender groups and sometimes as mixed groups or pairs. In addition to the filming, Pat also made observational notes in a research journal. These observations might record play scenarios, or group times, or arrival and departure times in the unit, or, as stated above, conversations with the team members or perhaps with parents. Although it was not possible to film everything, it did seem important to try and capture events that made up the day and that provided opportunities for subsequent viewing and joint reflection. If we were going to be successful in eliciting the pedagogies that supported playful learning, and to better understand what playful learning looked like, we needed to try and capture as much as possible of the whole day/experiences of the children in order to try and understand the bigger picture of their playful learning lives in this early years unit.

From the outset, we set the work up as a research project gaining permissions from the head teacher (who was very supportive), the unit staff, the parents and, of course, the children. In a letter to parents we informed them that we would be filming the children but only for the purposes of the research; the films would not be shown elsewhere. They would be used to show the children and for the early years team to review and reflect upon. Parents were invited to return a slip to school if they did not want their children to be filmed but none did so.

The children were told who Pat was and what she was doing and that if they did not want Pat to do the filming they could ask her to stop. It was a delicate balance between giving children their rights to stop the filming and having them abandon their play in order to dance or sing for the camera, but gradually normal patterns of play developed and could be openly filmed. On one occasion, Pat was filming two girls who had gone to the coat area to get something from their pockets. It became apparent that there was clearly something 'secret' about their interaction and, although they did not ask for filming to stop, they looked with some dismay at the camera and at Pat and tried to hide their objects (lipsticks). It seemed important to respect their privacy and to withdraw quickly from the area, taking account of their indirect rather than direct request to stop filming. At any time in filming, if a child looked anxiously at the camera, the filming process moved away. We are aware of the considerable debates there now, quite rightly, are about the complexity of gaining assent and consent from children and the levels of competence children have when engaging with these processes

(Ramsden and Jones 2010). Even quite young children can, under the right circumstances, understand both the research process and their rights to give or withhold consent (Armistead 2010). Such research must also acknowledge the importance of sensitivity when entering children's worlds (Cosaro and Molinari 2001). The importance of both listening to and hearing children's voices and views has become an important part of research methodology in recent years (Clark and Moss 2001; Roberts 2001; Webster and Broadhead 2010).

The size of the modern camera was helpful in remaining 'invisible'. No longer do we need to raise them to our eyes and adopt a filming posture. The camera is small in size and, by using the screen tilted upwards, it was possible to sit and film the play without looking at the children on many occasions. Nevertheless, children would sometimes approach Pat and check whether filming was ongoing and Pat was always honest with them; however, they seemed generally unconcerned overall. The staff and the children in the unit use both digital and film cameras and the children seem to see their presence as a normal part of their daily routines. We elected not to put microphones on the children. In taking a naturalistic and spontaneous approach to filming, we did not know in advance who would be filmed. To have 'miked them up' once selected would have been highly invasive and likely to significantly change the spontaneous and absorbed aspects of their play. Consequently we did not always capture dialogue but did capture it on many occasions.

Watching the films with the children posed some challenges that we had not anticipated. There was not a lot of time available to us to engage in this aspect as we did not want to stop the play to do it and it needed to be done fairly quickly after the event to try and 'capture the moment' with the children. There were some periods such as general tidying and preparations for lunch and story time that could be used. However, another challenge was finding a space where we could set up the camera to play it onto a whiteboard and provide a large enough picture for the children to engage with. Although the unit did have an additional room and this was where we located the activity, the room was often also used by mothers and toddlers and for small group work so was not always available. These logistics probably meant that we did not engage with the children as often as we had thought we would but nevertheless a number of interesting discussions did take place and, where appropriate, these are incorporated in the book.

At first, when children realised they would be watching the films, they might ask suddenly during the play 'Can we watch it now?' but could usually be persuaded to wait until the end of the session. In this way, their desires could be respected and the play could continue its progress. The intention had been to invite specific children to talk about their play and on some occasions this could be achieved. However, on other occasions, when children realised that two or three children were going to watch the film, a larger group would ask if they could come and it seemed appropriate to allow them to do so as there was seldom time to watch the films more than once in the busy day. On these occasions, it was much harder to record the dialogue in response to the filming and indeed even when only two or three children were watching it became apparent that taping their responses was useless as their voices were drowned out by the voices on film. Consequently, it was necessary to write their responses as rapidly as possible which inevitably meant that some conversations were difficult to capture in their entirety.

So, there were quite a few logistics related to the filming aspect that we had not foreseen and that we needed to work around to both progress the study and respect the children's rights, interests and requests.

The early years team members were interviewed individually about the development of their careers and their feelings about how the provision was developing in its exploration of open-ended play and in relation to other aspects such as responses from other staff members outside the unit, challenges and strengths, likes and dislikes. They were assured of confidentiality and their transcripts were returned to them to see if they wished to delete any statements that might subsequently be used in the book. None of them made deletions and they have seen copies of the developing chapters. The staff team selected their own research names and each of them, of their own volition, gave copies of their transcript to Andy to read.

Informal conversations were undertaken with parents, including new parents who were visiting the setting. These were recorded by Pat in her journal as soon as possible after the conversation was finished. Pat would introduce herself and explain the work that was being undertaken as a lead in to questions around initial responses to and feelings about the setting. In addition, the staff also reported several conversations they had undertaken with parents and the general responses of parents – both positive and negative – to the setting when the children started and as they settled in. We have built these into the book as well, where possible.

'To play or not to play' – or just to 'play a little bit': the influence of theory and policy on decision-making for early years educators

This final section looks briefly at the kinds of pressures and expectations that there have been across the early years in relation to 'letting children play' and links this with some reflections on the theoretical ideas that have or are framing our understanding of play, its purposes and its expression in young children's lives, at this point in time. These policy/theory frames run through the chapters of the book and are also reconsidered in the final chapter as we look to the possible future for playful learning and playful pedagogies in early years settings.

Playful approaches have a very well-established pedigree in the early years literature across the UK and until quite recently these were framed within child development approaches (or DAP as it has come to be known – Developmentally Appropriate Practice). These have been guided and informed most substantially by Piaget's work. Piaget led the way in relation to promoting active learning, of which 'play' was seen as a central approach and often linked with terms such as 'discovery learning' and 'child-centred' learning. During the 1970s and 1980s when Piagetian philosophies were at their peak in the UK, play, active learning and discovery learning featured also as policy drivers and were supported as important and central approaches across the early years of education and service provision. The Plowden Report (CACE 1967) drew substantially on Piagetian theory and was undoubtedly influential during the 1970s and early 1980s in changing the ethos of some primary schools to 'active' and 'discovery' learning and putting the child in the position of leader of her/his own learning. In relation to the primary curriculum, these ideas were reframed quite extensively in the Rose Review (DCSF 2009a) of the primary curriculum, implemented by the then Labour government but subsequently sidelined and dismissed by the Conservative/Liberal Democrat coalition government coming into power in 2010. Ideas about and conceptualisations of 'active learning' as depicted and developed in Piagetian learning theory are not, so far it seems, to be permanently submerged from view and are certainly kept alive in early years philosophies and practices.

It is important to recall that during the 1970s and 1980s, when these ideas were 'taking hold' in England, there was no centralised curriculum and schools and teachers had substantial freedoms in determining the daily curricular experiences of children; the National Curriculum was not to emerge until the Education Act of 1988. This high level of curricular freedom, along with a prevailing policy view around active/experiential learning, resulted in a correspondingly high status for play and playful approaches in early years educational settings. However, play was not always well understood by practitioners (Bennett *et al.* 1997; Wood and Attfield 2005) even whilst it was seen as essential in supporting young learners (Anning 1997; Bruce 1987; Moyles 1989). Play, especially for younger children, was seen as the norm in this period, and staff were seldom called upon to defend its worth as integral to learning processes.

These 'active' and 'playful' approaches were being substantially criticised in the late 1970s and early 1980s, most notably as a result of a set of papers called the Black Papers (Cox and Dyson 1971). Leading on from these debates around the influence of what were termed 'progressive educational ideas' the introduction of the National Curriculum in 1988 brought about a profound change across educational provision in England, a change that was to have a substantial and long-term impact on the previously high status of play and in particular on the experiences of reception-aged children. There was already some research to show that not all of this age group were experiencing well-developed playful learning environments (Bennett and Kell 1989; Cleave and Brown 1991) and continuing studies would show that this trend was exacerbated by subsequent curriculum and assessment initiatives (Adams *et al.* 2004; Anning and Edwards 1999).

Over time, this increasingly centralised control of the curriculum and, of course, associated testing has impacted in detrimental ways upon playful provision both in educational settings and in the expanding services emerging from the private and voluntary sectors for young children and families, by creating a culture both of performativity and surveillance (David *et al*. 2010). This, for the first time in England, was a centralised curriculum, subject to testing arrangements and forming the basis for league tables which compared school with school from the mid-1990s onwards. In keeping with this growing trend of accountability and an emphasis on summative assessment, from 1998 onwards, schools were originally expected to baseline-assess their reception-aged children within the first few weeks of entry into the reception class. This created huge pressures for staff trying to settle four-year-olds to new routines and spaces without the generosity of staffing ratios they would have had in a nursery setting for children of the same age (still four years old). It inculcated an ethos of 'testing' with children expected to be seated with an adult for the purpose of the 'testing'.

At this point, there was no Foundation Stage Curriculum; this would not emerge until the year 2000 for three- to five-year-olds (QCA 2000), and Local Authorities were each devising their own Baseline Assessment 'tasks'. This initiative created an ethos of formal testing for newly admitted reception children and inevitably diminished practitioner's engagements with playful approaches, especially in reception classrooms (Adams *et al*. 2004; Broadhead 2004). The Foundation Stage Profile (QCA 2003) brought a national framework for pupil assessment to be completed by the end of the Foundation Stage (the reception class year) but the ethos of testing and of box-ticking was established and it was difficult to reconcile this with an ethos of choice and decision-making that emerged from children's interests, experiences and discoveries. To cap it all, the National Literacy and Numeracy Strategies were taking up much of the day in many reception classrooms, and play became the 'Golden Time' of Friday afternoons (Brooker 2010), rather than a daily engagement with child-initiated activities. This policy ethos influenced not only reception teachers and teams but also had downwards influence across the staff in nursery classes in schools and in the private and voluntary sectors, who were increasingly being required to 'prepare children' for school. The ethos of education and of learning in these years since 1988 had been mainly teacher-led and adult-dominated except for any pockets of practice across the sector that kept the faith with play (Anning and Edwards 1999). However, even for these practitioners, wherever their setting, there would have been very few opportunities for their own professional development in relation to understanding play and learning because, by and large, it was off the agenda.

Still, there were academics, researchers and practitioners writing and publishing around play in the early years during this period and their work has been a source of inspiration to many who were struggling to sustain playful practices, especially in reception classrooms, where head teachers might be more concerned with 'results' than with sustaining playful approaches, and also concerned with the related implications for sustaining pupil numbers and the related budget in the competitive world of the school marketplace. As Henricks (2010: 195) states: 'Adults routinely judge children to be 'at play' because they see no consequences for the activity beyond the event itself'. In the perceived absence of 'outcome' the play activity is often deemed low status. Having said this, there were some heads in this period and since who have valued play and have seen and understood its positive impact on children's learning, behaviour and growth, and there were also heads who trusted their early years staff sufficiently to let them develop the provision in the way that they believed best met the children's needs even though they might not, as heads, have been able to articulate the benefits themselves.

From the mid-1990s onwards, Vygotsky's theoretical perspectives on children, learning and play began to have greater impact on research and publications, and many practitioners have come across his ideas around the Zone of Proximal Development as a way of thinking about how children make progress in their learning (Vygotsky 1966, 1986). Vygotsky placed a strong emphasis on the role of the environment in relation to intellectual development, more so than Piaget, who had seen intellectual development most substantially as a maturational process and thought little about contextual impact arising from such aspects as the time available for play, access to materials and the adult's role. Vygotsky also developed ideas around the impact of social interactions between adults and children as contributing to individual development but within wider communities of learners – not as solitary action. This has led researchers to look more closely at children's interactions with other children, at how they use the materials and objects available to them, at how they pursue their interests when able to do so and at the decisions that adults take in relation to children's own decisions for action. All of these and others are approaches that have been especially important within the research reported in this book (see also Pramling-Samuelsson and Fleer 2009).

What we have also tried to do in the book is to illustrate some ways in which adults might make sense of the play themes and interests that children bring to their play when they are free to theme it themselves and without adult direction – but not necessarily without adult engagement. Leading on from Vygotsky's and others' work in this area has been a more recent and well-developed movement that has much more substantially developed socio-cultural approaches to teaching and learning in the early years. Rogoff's work around communities of learners and the cultural nature of human development (Rogoff 1990, 1994, 2003) urged consideration of the child's development in relation to interactions with other participants engaged within the activity and the wider community of learners within which the activity is located; the community may be that of home or school. Fleer (2002), Fleer and Richardson (2004) and Edwards (2006, 2009) illustrate how socio-cultural theory sees development as dependent on the social and cultural experiences of the child and not as a 'universal and unvarying process' depicted by theories of child development (DAP) (Edwards 2009: 13). However, these too have evolved in recent years to incorporate the influences of the child's contextualised experiences on the learning process (Whitebread 2002).

How then does the educator take this into account in creating and sustaining a playful learning environment for many children? How is it possible to think of each child as 'unique' when there are so many in the setting? One of the ideas we explore in this book is that children may not be so unique, that in fact they have many interests in common with other children (although not necessarily with all children) and can express and explore these common and shared interests in the right environment and with adults who understand the power of self-expression through playful learning.

Although Vygotsky's work and the related theoretical positions leading on from it were being influential in the development of theoretical ideas about children's learning through play, it had had relatively little impact on early years policy development in England until the 'dying moments' of Labour's term of office in 2010. The Curriculum Guidance for the Foundation Stage (QCA 2000) had been superseded in 2007 by the Early Years Foundation Stage (EYFS) for children aged from birth to five years (DfES 2007). A significant part of the practice guidance for the EYFS was still most substantially rooted within an individual, developmental model, aligned with specified and individualised developmental outcomes, or the *Early Learning Goals* as they were named. The EYFS does make more extensive references to play than did the 2000 curriculum document and there are parts of it that hint at moves from individual, developmental models in the relatively brief sections that relate to play in the Practice Guidance and in the Principle into Practice Cards.

These aspects were perhaps more substantially developed in subsequent guidance documents that emerged after 2007 and which formed the basis for much of the regional and local early years training ongoing across the country. These materials (DCSF 2009b, 2009c) signalled some shifts towards the adoption of socio-cultural approaches in policy and certainly aimed at locating play much more centrally at the heart of good early years practice. However, the DCSF (2009b: 5) still associated play with 'unstructured' activity, and claimed that it can at times be 'chaotic or repetitive activity' and by this token, apparently, has less value in relation to young children's learning. However, practitioners welcomed the EYFS as a major influence on practice and in supporting play-based and child-led activities but also expressed a need for more professional development opportunities relating to its implementation (Aubrey 2004; Brooker *et al.* 2010)

A key debate that emerged from the EPPE study (Sylva *et al.* 2010) and which is addressed further and in more detail in the published practice guidance (DCSF 2009b) relates to creating and sustaining a balance between *teacher-directed activity* in the early years and *child-initiated activity*. The recognition that children's interests and themes emerge from their self-initiated play seemed broadly accepted in this policy guidance but whether and how that can serve to change the tide of practice established since 1988 remains to be seen. Much of this debate around teacher-directed and child-initiated learning seems to focus on whether and how adults can lead playful activity *as a tool* for promoting learning rather than having the potential to create opportunities for playful learning as arising from children's interests and experiences.

This is a central issue for this book as we try, in the following chapters, to share with you a model that has this question at its heart but has tried to address it in a far more sophisticated way than, for example, allocations of time in a day or a week to each of teacher-directed and child-initiated activity. Rather, it seeks to put playful learning and playful pedagogies at the heart of the children's day-to-day learning experiences and only then to decide whether, when and how to incorporate teacher-led group work or to address approaches to adult engagement with play. Although the group work may have playful pedagogical elements, it is not called play; there is no sense of play being 'harnessed' in order to 'teach' but, perhaps most importantly of all, there is a clear sense of play as a powerful learning mode for both children and adults. The challenge is to understand it better than we do, and perhaps also to accept the fact that much of what children learn through play may never be evident to adults, no matter how many observations they undertake. We hope this book can help in this search for a better understanding but we do not promise to have all the answers. We are, however, in agreement with Reynolds and Jones (1997: 77), who write:

> Direct teaching and rote learning in early childhood fail to ensure lasting school success, even when they produce temporary test results, because they provide an inadequate base for the higher order thinking skills that are needed in later schooling and in adult life. These skills have their foundation in play – in initiative taking, problem solving, and innovating within the constraints of reality.

We ask the reader to keep another model in mind as you read this book. We want to return to the two terms 'open-ended play' (we are deliberately avoiding the use of the word 'role' as in 'role play' because not all children's play is about role-taking – rather, we would argue, it is about internalising life-experiences) and 'the whatever you want it to be place' (a term which you may recall was 'created' by a reception child). At this stage, the model is presented very simply as in Table 0.1. The box on the left of the model represents a simplified account or summary of *playful pedagogy* whereas the box on the right tries to capture the essence of *playful learning*. The challenge for the book, then, is to try and illustrate the links between them as a conceptual 'whole' that can be created and sustained in an early years educational setting.

As this book was going to press, the recommendations from the Tickell review of the Early Years Foundation Stage, under the auspices of Michael Gove as Secretary of State for Education in the coalition government, had just been

Table 0.1 Playful pedagogies and playful learning: the juxtaposition model

'Open-ended play': understanding playful pedagogies	'The whatever you want it to be place': revealing playful learning
A way for the adult to conceive of her/his own role in creating and sustaining an educational environment that is flexible enough to allow children's interests and experiences to emerge and develop; it also encompasses the adults' responsibilities in identifying, recording and planning for those interests in systematic but flexible ways and a responsibility to look for ways of extending those interests and relating them to the wider world in which the child is living and learning. The early years setting becomes a space and place where adults nurture potential and push the boundaries of their personal understandings of playful learning and playful pedagogies.	The environment and its possibilities as perceived and engaged with from the child's perspective. The child enters a space where anything is possible – whether a large or small space – and where they can engage alone or with others in exploring and exploiting that environment to match the images, plans and memories that emerge from their own minds, experiences and skills. The early years setting becomes a space and place where children explore their identity, potential and interests and push back the boundaries of personal possibility through playful engagement.

published for consultation. We return to consider this latest aspect of early years curriculum development and potential impact in Chapter 7 of the book but let us move now into the outdoor area at Fishergate early years unit.

Chapter 2

Resourcing and developing playful learning environments

The outdoor area

The chapter begins by examining the experiences and perspectives of the staff team at Fishergate and considers this in relation to wider perspectives on changing practice in the early years. We look at the impetus for and influences on the changes that began to occur in the outdoor area. We then present three extended vignettes of children's play in the outdoor area to show the competences and complexities of the play and the children's engagements with the open-ended resources.

The vignettes have been linked with the Early Learning Goals. These are found in the *Development Matters* column in the EYFS (DfES 2007) and presented there in bold print. Three or four outcomes are provided for each vignette to show that open-ended play in the 'whatever you want it to be place' corresponds closely with opportunities to achieve learning outcomes. It would have been possible to have provided more in several cases. Although we are at a point in time when it is likely that the EYFS will reduce in content (although we do not know for sure and will return to this in the final chapter), nevertheless, early years educators will be working to a specified curriculum that will undoubtedly be linked to learning outcomes of some kind. We want to illustrate how, when children lead their play in the right kind of learning environment, with the right kind of adult support, they are capable of making progress that accords with the curriculum. These vignettes also illustrate how much richer and more complex the children's playful learning is, more so than anything depicted by decontextualised learning outcomes as determined by adults. This progression through play becomes more evident when children are playing together because it is through their actions, interactions and language that learning and understanding are revealed to the observer.

Changing practices in the outdoor area at Fishergate

In this introductory reflection Debbie reveals the extent of her own developmental journey over time, illustrating a shift from a personal sense of uncertainty to one of personal and professional achievement. She also shows how she has come to understand the extent to which she had previously underestimated the children's capacities for taking on board new ways of being in a changing early years environment. Debbie is reflecting here on suggestions to change the outdoor environment, which this chapter will focus on in further detail:

> It's turned around quickly, I didn't think it would turn around so quickly but it's turned around from the adult leading to the child leading. Faster than I thought. How can we do this? What shall we do? Turning those questions back to the child has turned it all around really quickly. When Andy first suggested child-led learning I thought it's going to take them a long time to get used to this. I thought it would take me a long time but it didn't. It took me a few months, maybe a couple of terms and then I thought 'wow'.

In the following chapters, as well as drawing from the reflections of the wider staff team, we will also include some extended reflections from Andy and occasionally from Pat. We want to try and convey the sense of changes over time in relation to new approaches to teaching and learning. If early years practitioners want to change the way they act (teach), Andy's and his colleagues' experiences show that they also have to be prepared to change the way they think about playful learning. The shifts in practice mirror their shifts in thinking. Chapter 1 noted that pedagogy is not just about what is done but is also about why the practitioner does what she/he does: where do the ideas come from? How are they framed? What influences the thinking and doing? The team in the unit have been engaged in a joint enterprise and, as we shall see as the book unfolds, although the broad principle of 'following the child's interests' is upheld by all the staff team, they do not necessarily always agree on actual practices and approaches and do not always have the same interpretations of what it means to 'follow the child's interests'. What they do have however is a shared understanding of how the environment nurtures children's interests, and this is what we are exploring in this and the next chapter.

Changing practice is a dynamic process; it is a living process and sometimes it may be a painful or challenging process. Sometimes, what we think we are doing is not what is actually being achieved. Maynard and Chicken (2010: 36) spoke of teachers in their project who acknowledged difficulty in moving away from a 'lens of targets and outcomes'; Chapter 1 explored the ethos that created and sustained this expectation. Although Maynard and Chicken's teachers thought they were giving children more autonomy in the classroom, the research revealed that the teachers were in effect only increasing the number of content-focussed, planned activities available to the children to choose from during the session. 'Autonomy' is a relative term and the vignettes we have selected for this chapter are hoping to depict real and very evident autonomy in children's play.

Three vignettes have been selected for discussion in this chapter. None of them includes direct adult intervention, although of course adults are involved pedagogically because they have resourced the environment and created the space and time for children to engage with their peers in this environment.

What has emerged in Fishergate is that the inspiration for continuing the movement towards more open-ended play provision is what the staff see in terms of the children's responses to the changing environment; this deep immersion and continual engagement with problem-setting and problem-solving by the children is what we have tried to depict in these vignettes and so the vignettes are not short ones. As evidence of children's absorption, increased creativity and problem-solving emerged, so the team felt more confident in changing their approaches to learning and teaching through playful provision; changes in teaching and in learning opportunities ran in parallel. However, we should also state that for a new member of staff, Vicky, there were also some initial concerns that she tuned into as new children settled in, an early days 'wondering about' how the benefits might eventually look, as she reflected:

> I don't feel that the space is too open-ended but I sometimes feel . . . some-times I struggle with the messiness of it all. It seems a bit like . . . it's that balance of what we provide, how they practise and what we use. It's partly my own thing of how I like things to be tidy and neat but also I know that my own children like to access things that are usable. If you go to get a pen, it works and there's not loads of broken bits. That's quite hard for a practitioner to keep it looking like that.

Vicky's view is legitimate in terms of her own concept of how the space might look and how or whether she can come to accommodate what, to her, feels like 'messiness' in this early phase of her engagement with the unit.

Moving towards more open-ended approaches in the outdoor area

Andy reflects:

> The beginnings of our open-ended approach in the early years unit emerged in 2006 and, from there, gradually evolved over the following years. In these days, before the EYFS, our planning had been focussed on providing activi-ties which were linked to the objectives taken from the Stepping Stones within the Curriculum Guidance for the Foundation Stage. These activi-ties were delivered to the children through half-termly topics. In this way, six topics would be delivered through the school year. A two-year rolling programme of topics ensured that all of the areas of the curriculum were covered. This was in keeping with practice more broadly across the Local Authority. Alongside this rolling programme of topics, focussed planning for literacy with phonics and numeracy provided other teacher-led activities in keeping with the National Strategies. Additionally and on a daily basis,

focussed group activities linked to the topic ran throughout the session.

To some extent, this approach was working. The Ofsted report in 2006 had said that significant improvements had been made to the early years unit during the previous 18 months. It said that our provision was good and children were making good progress.

The indoor area had clearly defined areas of provision such as the home corner, a role play area linked to the topic, large and small construction, sand, water, painting, writing and drawing, etc. It looked very similar to any other setting and the Ofsted inspector, noting the strengths of the indoor area, asked what we were going to focus on next in our ongoing develop-ment. I replied that I felt it was time to further develop the outdoor space and to move on from more or less replicating the indoor space with a few additional bikes, etc. This recommendation appeared in the report saying that we should maximise the potential of the Foundation Stage outdoor play area so that it provided more learning opportunities. This area then became a focus of the team's attention.

Also at this time, I began attending a year-long course focussing on early years practice and was out of the unit for two days a term, looking at other settings, getting new ideas and reflecting with colleagues. Looking back now, I can see how important this period of reflection and learning was for me; my focus of development became the outdoor play.

As the team began to talk about and work on the development of the outdoor area, it was becoming clear that there was gradually less enthusi-asm for the topic-based approach. We were finding that the outdoor area was being led by the children's interests whereas the indoors was still being driven by topic-related planning. The topic-based approach required a great deal of planning time and the curricular repetition seemed increasingly less interesting for staff so it became harder to think about enthusing the children. At this time, I was leading the planning, and then meeting time had to be taken in sharing the planning with the team, before the activities themselves could be undertaken with the children. This did not seem to be the best use of our precious time in terms of supporting the children's learning and development and at the time, we were recognising how much more interesting the outdoor play was starting to look. It was around this time that the first drafts of the EYFS were released. The arrival coincided well with our developing work outdoors that was now being built around using children's interests as the starting point for learning.

Outdoor play: a broader perspective

We can see that Andy and the team were being influenced by Andy's profes-sional development experiences but it might also be claimed that a number of other factors were coming together from the wider society around the team and from other cultural influences. Part of this was a 'swell' in this period in relation to some aspects of outdoor play. There had been growing and wider societal concerns about children no longer playing outside owing to fears of abduction (Furedi 2002; Gill 2006) with no actual evidence of any increase in the dangers of the outdoors (Tovey 2007). Over time, these concerns had become linked to other concerns around obesity and changing lifestyles that tended not to include exercise for children (O'Dea and Erikson 2010). These emerging and ongoing concerns culminated in 2005 in the then Labour government's establishing Play England, funded by National Lottery money as part of the National Children's Bureau. Play England advised Local Authorities in establishing outdoor play spaces in parks and public areas from central government funding. The Labour government had made £235 million available for national playground development through the Playbuilder scheme launched in 2008 and aiming to provide 3,500 community playgrounds across England. This initiative had little influence on play provision in early years settings; nevertheless the establishing of a national body does raise status, and 'play' became a national issue during this period with an especially high and very welcome profile.

Despite these initiatives, however, Gleave (2010) in a survey commissioned by Play England found that almost one third of children between the ages of 7 and 14 had never played in the street, compared with 90 per cent of adults who had regularly played in the street as children. Then in 2010, the coalition government in its programme of cuts froze the Playbuilder scheme, which meant that any play areas which had not by then been developed in Local Authorities would not be developed; no further funds would be available and it seemed the status of play was beginning to diminish once again.

The concept of the 'outdoor classroom' had also emerged in the wider literature in mid-decade to parallel this national emphasis on outdoor developments (Education and Skills Committee 2005; Ofsted 2004). It was being taken onboard within the early years literature, in which outdoor play had always featured as integral to good practice (Isaacs, McMillan, Froebel, Rousseau and others were all early advocates). The Forest Schools movement gained ground in this period (Tovey 2007), urging access to woodland environments where children might climb trees, explore water, enjoy mud, use saws and knives and light fires.

The EYFS (DfES 2007: para 1.16), although bringing forward a higher profile for play overall, was however a little ambiguous on the issue of outdoor play, stating in the Practice Guidance:

> Play underpins the delivery of all the EYFS. Children must have opportunities to play indoors and outdoors. All early years providers must have access to an outdoor play area which can benefit the children. If a setting does not have direct access to an outdoor play area then they must make arrangements for daily opportunities for outdoor play in an appropriate nearby location.

This is a rather contradictory statement ('All must have' . . . 'If a setting does not have') and leaves the possibility of operating with young children with limited access to outdoor play, as Tovey (2007) notes from some settings she has visited. She also draws attention to research by Adams and colleagues (2004), who show that outdoor provision for reception-aged children can be variable and restrictive in some cases. Tovey also reminds us of the DES survey back in 1989, which noted even then that four-year-olds rarely had opportunities for outdoor play. So, although there may have been a changing climate relating to the wider status of play, up until 2010, the experiences of young children in early years settings still had a somewhat chequered history and initiatives such as Forest Schools had been comparatively limited with only local impact.

Andy continued his reflections:

> There were many reasons for developing the outdoor area. To begin with, the resources that were provided for the children were generally smaller resources such as cars on a mat or a train with small pieces of track. These resources were carried out of the outdoor sheds at the beginning of the day and left in the outdoor area for the children to use. Also, at one end of the outdoor area, a small wooden house with windows and a door and small furniture inside was presented as the focus for role play. As I became increasingly reflective, and read more about different approaches to outdoor play, it became clear to me that what we had been offering was not really very much different from many of the resources in the indoor area. As I came to see, the point of outdoor play is to offer something which is in nature very different from the indoor provision. To offer provision on the same scale with the same defined areas as indoors may well have adhered to the idea that the inside area should mirror the outdoor area, but it certainly didn't make the most of the freedom that having a large outdoor space can allow. In a large outdoor area it is possible to use resources which, because of their scale, would not be appropriate inside and it is this concept that the staff began to explore.

Bringing in new resources

The early years team discussed how the outdoor area could be redeveloped. It was not financially possible to completely redesign and rebuild the area, as many other schools were doing at the time, and the team therefore needed to think more creatively about what might be done. A simple plan of the outdoor space was drawn up with specific areas for different activities. There was to be an area for large construction, ball games and mark-making on large blackboards in addition to sand and water play. With hindsight, the team realised that they were still thinking quite traditionally about 'areas' as they planned the outdoor space. The greatest departure from the previous provision was in the materials that were to be provided in many of these areas. A list of the resources that the staff required was compiled. This included planks of wood, tyres of different sizes, tarpaulins, milk crates, drainpipes, guttering and hosepipes. A letter was sent out to all the parents in the school asking for donations of any of these resources. What the team did not realise at this stage of their planning was that these resources were not compatible with ideas about 'specific areas'. Two quite different philosophies were at work here but the outcome would eventually be very positive, if rather unexpected.

Andy continued:

> We were completely taken aback by the response from the parents. One of the dads, who was a builder, arrived at school with a huge collection of planks of wood. On another day an army truck drove into the school playground with three big truck tyres on the back. The father of one of the older children in the school was a soldier and his wife, a mid-day supervisor, had read our letter and mentioned that her husband could bring the tyres if we wanted them. The army also donated a tarpaulin which had previously been used as a cover for a tank. In our outdoor area it was to be used in more varied and creative ways by the children as part of their play. A local milk man donated twenty milk crates, and some sections of drainpipe, hosepipe and guttering were purchased from a DIY store. The nature of the way that the resources had been purchased and donated, the size and amount of resources meant that storage was a challenge. Piles of tyres, wooden planks and drainpipes festooned the outdoor area and that was after we had tidied up. We were still wondering how to store all these materials when we realised that the children had just started playing with them.

In the weeks that followed three large wooden boards were purchased, painted with blackboard paint and fixed onto the sheds and fences. The staff began observing the children and their use of the materials and realised their effect on the children's play was powerful. Perhaps because there was no pre-determined expectation by the adults as to how the resources were to be used, the children just picked up the materials and explored them in many different ways; the children led the play, they did not need anything explaining. The team began to notice and discuss the following:

- The play was more physical, energetic, noisy and mobile.
- The play was not just located in one area; as well as moving around the outdoor area the play was also taken indoors. The team remarked that the play was more fluid and the play themes more prolonged than previously.
- At first, the staff felt that the play, although interesting, seemed more chaotic and frenetic. Discussions about risk and safety began but no one wanted to stop the play and children were not getting hurt. Observations showed that children were approaching the materials carefully, although once they were confident there was more physical engagement and risk-taking.
- The children seemed to be much more engaged, with play going on for long periods of time, and deep absorption and concentration being evident.

- One team member expressed concerns that some children, particularly the younger girls and boys, seemed reluctant to go outdoors. This prompted staff to think about and begin to monitor who was and was not going outside.
- What they then noted was that younger and older children used the resources in different ways, at their own levels of confidence and skill and for different periods of time.

The outdoor area 2011: how did it look?

The outdoor area in the unit is a portioned-off section of the larger, primary playground with a low wooden fence around it and a tarmac surface (Figure 2.1 and Figure 2.2). Children have direct access, from the indoor area, throughout the day. The area is well hidden by a high wall around the school allowing many of the materials to be left out overnight. If the children have made something they wish to return to the next day, this can be accommodated. When it rains, the puddles that collect in the tarpaulins, for example, create new interests and new areas of focus for the play. The team began to notice how the weather influenced the play and the children's explorations of the environment. In the centre is a circular walled area with a raised flower bed, and additional flower beds and small garden areas are laid out to one side of the space. Flowers and vegetables

Figure 2.1 The outdoor area.

Figure 2.2 The outdoor area.

are planted and cared for by the children. There are two storage sheds. Three large blackboards are attached to the sheds and the perimeter fence. There is a large sandpit area that the children can walk into in an enclosed, low walled area although this is a more recent addition, provided by a father who is a builder. A pulley system has been created on one wall. The pulley system is close to an outdoor tap that is placed at child height. Other resources are listed in Table 2.1.

A range of art and drawing materials are regularly available outdoors such as chalk, powder paints and brushes. The children are allowed to paint on walls and windows with powder paint and on floors and resources if they wish. What Andy and the team have created here, over time, fits well with the concepts and ideas of 'Loose Parts', although this term was not familiar to them while these ideas were developing and the outdoor learning environment was changing from 2006 onwards.

Loose Parts Theory originated through the work of the architect Simon Nicholson (1971) and advocates the value of open-ended play materials to accord with the ideas and possibilities that develop in children's minds as they play. It has been further developed most substantially in the Playwork Literature. Taylor (2008) gives a clear historical account of its development through Nicholson's work. Nicholson observed the building of children's playgrounds in the 1960s and commented that, whereas children played there when they were under construction, they ceased to do so once they were complete; there

Table 2.1 Resources in the outdoor area

Made materials	Natural materials
9 builders' sacks	Around 30 wooden planks of
2 builders' trays	varying lengths and thicknesses
5 tarpaulins of different sizes	11 tree branches and stumps
24 tyres of various sizes	Differently sized stones and
Lengths of guttering and drainpipe	pebbles
Pieces of rope of varying lengths	Soil, one tree in the central area,
Plastic tubing of various widths and lengths –	bulbs, vegetables and plants
some that children can crawl through, some	with the seasons
that bend, some straight, some curved	Insects, spiders, woodlice etc.
12 bread trays	The seasons
30 milk crates	Puddles and rain
1 water tray	Wind
10 cable reels	Snow and ice
Large selection of wooden blocks	
15 large, plastic water containers	
Purpose designed wire stands to support	
guttering at child height for water exploration	

was no longer any challenge or interest in the adult-themed pre-determined spaces they had become. The Theory of Loose Parts states that 'In any environment both the degree of inventiveness and creativity and the possibility of discovery are directly proportional to the number and kinds of variables in it' (Nicholson 1971: 30). Brown (2003) has also written about the Theory of Loose Parts, stating: 'flexibility in the play environment leads to increased flexibility in the child. The child is then better able to make use of the flexible environment . . . and moves closer to their developmental potential than would otherwise have been the case' (2003: 56–57). Each of these writers is describing outdoor, community-based, playful environments but with the 'whatever you want it to be place' we came to see that similar ideas had emerged from quite different reference points and age groups. However, these ideas have much in common in relation to allowing children to take control of their own play and their own learning in an early years educational setting, with which this book is concerned.

The Fishergate early years unit has also kept the bikes and scooters and similar materials; these are available to children at times and sometimes children request them and clearly enjoy using them. They combine them with ramps and planks and bridges and so explore momentum, speed and forces in quite natural ways.

Playing outdoors at Fishergate

One of the key issues for this book – and one of the most elusive – is in trying to illustrate how and what children learn in their open-ended play. The final paragraph of Chapter 1 presented a simple model that drew a distinction between two terms used for describing these spaces and the activities within them. We spoke of adults pedagogically concerned with providing *open-ended play* opportunities (also termed 'Loose Parts' in this chapter) whereas for the children, the concept of the *whatever you want it to be place* seems more readily to speak their language – being indeed the language of one young girl in response to her teacher's quandary about what they should call the open-ended play area.

In presenting and reflecting on the forthcoming play vignettes, we aim to try and unpack the play from both children's and adults' perspectives to try and see the relationships between learning and pedagogy.

Vignette I

Archie and Luke; progression in play – from small to large enclosure design

This first vignette took place when Archie and Luke were young four-year-olds and had started to show an interest in playing together outdoors; when they watched the film after playing they said that this was the first time they had played at 'this'. It was not to be the last time. The filming lasted 20 minutes but the two boys were playing together before filming began. As the vignettes are presented, the play is described first of all, followed by reflections and interpretations from Andy and Pat. Where children have viewed and commented on the film, their comments are also included, as are those of other team members when available.

Archie and Luke have made an enclosure outside with small, shallow plastic crates – the type used for mushroom delivery to shops. It is quite a small enclosure and the two of them can just get in it, side by side. Archie has a small box, a pine cone and a stone carefully placed on the low wall that forms part of the enclosure and is using them within one corner of their space, adjusting their placements slightly and keeping up a running commentary, mostly to himself. Archie is focussed on this area for much of the play, sometimes leaving the area to fetch other small items – a stone, a feather. Luke says something about 'the toilet' and he is focussed on a small construction in one corner at the side of Archie. Archie collects soil from a little pile just outside the enclosure and places it carefully in an aerosol top, then taking it to his collection of objects on the wall. Luke has been across to the tap to fetch water in a small plastic container. He 'sits' on the toilet, quite absorbed; Archie looks and laughs gently at him, Luke returns a smile. Archie has found a piece of paper which he takes to his collection of objects. Luke pours water into the 'toilet'. There are two 'doors' (crates poised on their narrow ends) in the construction and Luke and Archie are always very careful to 'open and close' these as they leave and enter. Luke goes to dig in the soil that Archie has been digging in. In his space, Archie is still carefully manipulating small piles of soil and looks carefully at stones and his piece of paper. Luke has found a woodlouse in the soil and studies its movements for several minutes before returning to his digging.

EYFS learning outcomes

PSRN: Use and develop mathematical ideas and methods to solve practical problems.

KUW: Build and construct a wide range of objects, select appropriate resources, adapting their work where necessary.

PD: Recognise the importance of keeping healthy and those things which contribute to it (most evident in the post-play conversation between Archie and Luke).

Reflecting on the play

In this vignette, the boys seem, on first reflection, to be engaged in the parallel play characteristic of much younger children. However, further interrogation of the filmed material reveals that the play has strong cooperative elements with linked play themes and shared goals. These might not be apparent to a casual observer because relatively little language is exchanged between the boys although they do regularly interact. They have together designed a space within which home-related themes can be enacted. Luke's themes are toilet focussed; he makes this clear when he watches the film afterwards and, as they watch the film, he and Archie continue to find shared humour in the idea of 'going to the toilet'. Of course, toilet humour preoccupies adults too. However, Luke expands on this to say he is also cleaning the toilet with bleach (the trip to the tap – and bleach is a dangerous substance; we might imagine conversations he has had with a parent using bleach) and that he is flushing the toilet and at one point he states that he 'needs a stick to clean the toilet'. Chatting to one another as they watch the film, Luke comments very seriously to Archie, who is also serious in his response, that 'you have to wipe your bum when you go to the toilet'. These are important issues for Luke at this stage of his development; it seems that everything to do with toilets is of interest to him and, although not seemingly directly interested himself, Archie seems content to engage with Luke on this theme and also seems to recognise that it has a significance for Luke. Perhaps it had a similar significance for Archie not so long ago and remains a strong memory for him.

Although there seems to be very little language between Archie and Luke there is clearly a shared understanding of the purpose of the space; this may have developed prior to filming, when the boys were designing the space, although clearly, as they play, they are continuing to think about the purposes and uses of the space they have designed. Once agreed, the purpose does not have to be constantly referenced; it becomes part of who they are and of what they are doing together. Also, we might presume, they need time to think as they play, to draw on stored memories and experiences within their own homes to inform the development of their respective play events. Although the notion of domestic play is generically accepted as part of children's play, what Archie and Luke are showing us perhaps is that what happens in each home might be different for different children, or that they choose to focus on different aspects of home life as intellectually interesting for them. Archie never gives an explanation for his careful placing of objects but the actions are undoubtedly linked with images in his mind and with memories and experiences from home; the concentration is evident for both boys; they are completely absorbed in their companionable play and do not once notice they are being filmed. Because the whole outdoor space is so flexible, the boys make meaning from the objects they find – even pieces of paper – and interpret those meanings internally in ways that adults cannot necessarily access.

For both boys, the sense of boundaried space seems important; the creation of a space that they 'own' and can manipulate perhaps links to identity development as competent individuals growing increasingly able to manage their immediate environment rather than being dependent on adults to manage it for them, as they were when they were babies. This sense of identity and independence perhaps relates also to the mastering of toileting routines for Luke, something that no longer preoccupies Archie although it seems he can empathetically identify with it.

The end of the vignette noted Luke's interest in the woodlouse, which he came upon by accident. The staff's daily record for the previous days' activities outdoors had shown a huge interest, by quite a few children over several days, in things that crawl. The weather had been wet, and because of this the children had been finding snails and following snail trails. Several children had made homes for what they had found, using materials available indoors on a daily basis on the modelling table. Adults had engaged with them when requested and supported their writing activities as they had labelled the homes and looked at books on mini-beasts. Luke's examination of the woodlouse might seem a momentary activity unless it is placed in context of a more recent and wider focus on mini-beasts that had arisen spontaneously from the children's activities. We do not know, but perhaps, as he examined its movements, he was thinking back to conversations or activities he had participated in, in the previous days. His interest is clearly evident through his close observation of the woodlouse for several minutes.

Vignette 2

Archie and Luke: building on a bigger scale.

This second vignette takes place several months later when the boys are five years old. In between, Archie and Luke have often played together outdoors with the materials and there is no doubt that they have become expert players, their designs are complex. Rachel also remarked on having seen Archie's ongoing interest in 'design and build' and to have spent time with him on previous occasions in the outdoor area.

In this second vignette it can be seen that other children have started to take an interest in and to watch and then engage with the enclosures that Archie and Luke create; several such episodes have been captured on film. Not all of their play themes have been home-related although this seems to be a strong and continuing strand in their play together as is evident in this next extract.

This enclosure has been built from milk creates and takes up much more space than the previous design. It has a clearly designated 'corridor' about 15 feet long that leads into a 'room' that measures approximately eight feet around (Figure 2.3). The filmed material is very extensive, as the play continued for much of the morning session, although the film captures it at intervals, as other play is filmed at different times. The following are extracts from a much longer piece but still quite long because we feel there is much of interest here that relates to understanding the learning potential of the 'whatever you want it to be place'. It should be noted that, whenever the vignette refers to the 'door', this is a crate that children open and close in door-like fashion in a similar way to their play several months previously. Doors are important, it seems, and their design and use seems to be a constant in many children's open-ended play.

Archie has fetched two more milk crates and says to Luke: 'I want to make that thing where this leans up like that, do you remember that?' Luke seems unsure and asks where they will go. Archie says they will fit in the house and comes in with them. Luke is seated and watches. There is also a crate attached to the wall behind Luke's head and a small collection of artefacts carefully arranged beside it. Archie lays a crate on the floor and places the other inside it to make a slope. Luke climbs

Figure 2.3 The design begins with the corridor. Sebastian in his pirate hat is watching but, as the vignette reveals, Sebastian is not allowed to enter the play.

into it and lies down. Archie climbs in beside him and they smile at one another. They both climb out and Luke announces 'I'm cleaning, Archie. I'm cleaning'; he is using a small pot with water in and a small twig from a pine tree. Archie walks around the outdoor area, seemingly searching.

Barney (a new three-year-old) is shaking water on the room boundary (previous film has recorded him engaged with a magic theme – the water is a magic potion). Luke shouts 'Heyyyyyyy' at him and looks angry. Barney continues and does not seem aware of Luke. Patience (also playing at magic potions) was copying the action but she notices Luke's anger and stops and looks at him. Luke playfully hits Patience with his small twig and smiles; she does not smile back but does not seem concerned. Two younger children (Sebastian and friend) try to enter the construction through the door and down the corridor. Luke tries to block them and pushes them back out. They move away, unperturbed. Archie returns and enters via the door and down the corridor, closing the door behind him. He gives a jar of water to Luke, who begins his chores again; Archie has dipped Luke's twig into the water for him. Another boy comes with

a 'potion' to spread and Luke tells him 'No' and looks angry. The boy
moves elsewhere. Luke says to Archie: 'Everyone's trying to come in.'
Archie tidies some of the displaced crates.

Patience enters down the corridor and looks around. Noah with
plastic bricks on his arm (he is a robot) is watching from 'outside'.
He says 'I want to come in' and stamps his foot. Archie looks at him
and then enquiringly at Luke seated on the bed; they are discussing
this request and looking at Noah, who enters through the door and
down the corridor. He walks in and skips around the room. Luke looks
at him and says, 'No, no more people.' Archie says to him 'You can't
sleep here' and Luke says 'It's dark now.' Archie reiterates 'It's dark
now, you have to go back to your own house.' Luke says 'Our chairs
turn into beds', looks at Archie and laughs. Luke says to Noah 'Go
out' but laughs at him. Noah looks at Luke and does another little
skip and dance. Sebastian climbs in over the boundary and falls onto
the floor; all look at him. Sebastian walks around, looking. Luke and
Archie watch him. Sebastian walks along the corridor and back in again.
Luke and Archie are talking to Noah. Archie tells Sebastian to leave
and follows him out down the corridor and through the door, which
Archie closes. Noah goes to leave down the corridor but Archie invites
him back and he returns. Melinda has come to look at the construction from 'outside'. Archie gets into bed and stares quite angrily at
her. Sebastian is re-entering down the corridor. Archie looks anxiously
at Luke and then goes to tell Sebastian to leave and 'sees him out'
down the corridor for a second time. Melinda is still watching. Noah
has laid down on the floor to go to sleep. Melinda holds the door
open for Sebastian to leave and then closes it, staying outside. She
gently pushes Sebastian away, who runs off. Archie opens the door
for Melinda to enter. Sebastian has jumped back in over the boundary
wall and is posturing fight moves. Archie goes to him and calls 'No
swords in here everyone, no swords.' (Sebastian has his pirate hat on,
which he often does.) Archie says again to Sebastian 'No swords' and
Sebastian leaves – through the boundary. Archie returns the crates to
their proper place. Sebastian returns with a plank, which he throws into
the room. Melinda, Archie and Luke watch him but seem unconcerned.
Sebastian walks away, looking angrily back over his shoulder at them.
Luke removes the plank. Melinda announces she wants to go and leaves
with her two bags and high heels down the corridor. She announces she
is going on her holidays; Luke says 'Bye' and Noah waves and says 'We'll

see you tomorrow.' Luke waves and repeats 'We'll see you tomorrow.' Owen comes across and announces 'Luke, I want to go on holidays' and begins to arrange a large plastic shape onto its side beside the house. He climbs in and Luke laughs at him and stands to greet Archie as he returns through the door. Owen is inside the shape calling at Luke 'Hello, hello.' Later, Owen has entered the area. Luke and Archie are not present. Noah enters without his bricks and Owen shouts at him. Noah very obviously ignores him and walks calmly by. Noah is copying the cleaning/painting with water that Luke was doing earlier, by the 'television'. He is using Luke's pine twig. Owen leaves. Archie returns seeming very happy and holds something up: 'I've got my chandelier back. I thought I'd lost it.' Noah asks 'Where was it?' and Archie replies 'In the building corner.' He walks around as if looking where to place the miniature toy chandelier and chooses a spot on a crate very carefully. He continues the painting/cleaning with the twig. Noah goes to look at the chandelier. He picks up a small glass tube that is laid beside it and asks 'Where did you get this?' Archie does not answer but takes it from Noah, lays it back down again and returns to his cleaning. Melinda brings Rebecca into the enclosure through the door and Owen follows them, closing the door behind him. Archie looks at Owen, who says 'Archie, this door is shut.' Archie returns to his cleaning but then explains to Rebecca that 'this is a window so you can't go through there.' Rebecca looks and listens with interest, as does Melinda. Archie continues 'You can see through it.' Noah is still examining the glass tube, turning it around and looking through it. Owen talks to Archie and follows Melinda and Rebecca out along the corridor. Archie takes the glass tube and the chandelier to place in his pocket.

EYFS learning outcomes

KUW: Find out about their environment and talk about those features they like and dislike.

PD: Move with control and coordination.

CD: Use their imagination in art and design, music and dance, imagination, role play and stories. Explore colour, texture, shape, form and space in two or three dimensions.

Reflecting on the play

Throughout the year Archie has shown a very well-developed capacity for and interest in design and is the player who continues to change and recreate the spaces. Perhaps when he and Luke are designing, Archie can visualise the finished space more clearly. He certainly seems to be an expert player. Luke appears to be undertaking 'tasks' in much the same way he was in the earlier episode several months previously but, in keeping with the space they are now in, his activities also seem to be on a larger scale. The nature and function of the home seems to be mapped more clearly in their heads and this seems to allow them to work on this bigger scale. They seem to have a clear understanding of each other's skills and interests. We can see that they are still interested in the careful placing of objects but this aspect of their play has less prominence and the language has greater prominence as they have grown older and more experienced. Luke is no longer concerned with toilets but they now have included beds and windows in their play as well as corridors. Doors remain important to them; doors are generally how we enter and leave both new and familiar spaces and from a child's perspective perhaps represent objects of uncertainty; when young they must seldom know exactly what is on the other side of a closed door. Perhaps a regular engagement with the concept of 'door' helps them to diminish levels of uncertainly about new environments.

By this stage of the year, other children are clearly taking an interest in their play and in the space that Archie and Luke have created. Their play attracts younger children (Melinda, Rebecca and Barney, who are all relatively new to the unit) and other children who are still learning how to form relationships with their peers (Noah, Owen and Sebastian). Despite some earlier conflicts and protection of the space by both Luke and then Archie, only Sebastian is ultimately refused entry to the space. He is also the only one who seems unable at this stage to recognise the purpose of the 'door' and continually climbs over the boundary. Even Owen, an older, often solitary boy, has at one point reassured Archie that the door is 'closed' as if realising that this signals a willingness to be complicit with the rules of the play. Sebastian also has English as a second language so cannot as yet gain clues to the purpose of the space from listening to ongoing discussions and conversations. Sebastian expresses his anger at exclusion by throwing the plank but does not seem intent on hurting anyone and no one seems especially alarmed by this response although they do watch him carefully. Although Melinda does not stay long she shows a clear understanding of the playful purposes of the space and her departure introduces a new theme (holidays) that Owen can connect with. In this extract Owen shouts loudly and angrily at Noah, who deliberately ignores him; Owen does a great deal of shouting when frustrated and children have been advised by staff to 'try and ignore it' but he seems to connect with Melinda's holiday theme and a brief period of playful as opposed to watchful engagement – one that elicits a laugh from Luke with perhaps some positive reinforcement for Owen from this period of reciprocity. When Owen enters the space again he is accepted as a co-player and engages in conversation with Archie.

It is as if the creation of such play spaces by children also allows less skilful players to engage meaningfully at their own levels of skill and understanding; Archie and Luke are able to share their own, now expert, skills.

The extract shows the extent to which children are able to switch from real world to playful engagements – from planning to play, from searching to play, from conflict to play, from real-time conversation (about the chandelier) to play. Perhaps this does not even represent a 'switching' in their minds; this may be an adult construct. For them, it may be part of a continuous flow of being. This chandelier episode saw Noah in long and careful consideration of the small glass tube he found alongside the carefully placed miniature chandelier. What he was thinking is not evident; that he had found something of deep interest to him is very evident but who knows what he learned from this 'Loose Part' or what knowledge is framing in his mind as he looks and thinks? In some ways, it is reminiscent of Luke's observation of the woodlouse; a singular moment of deep meaning open only to the thinker.

An all-age and playful community: doing it in your own way at your own level but doing it together

Vignette 3

This play occurred just after Archie and Luke's large-scale play construction described above; in fact, as their play loses momentum, the children involved in this new activity begin to take some of the crates and materials that Archie and Luke have been playing with in order to extend their own construction.

In vignette 2, the final scenes we see on camera are Archie alone in the space, collecting and tidying sand that has been spilled on the floor by another child. Some crates have already been taken and he stands and watches the newly emerging play for a while before cleaning his hands on his jumper, leaving the area and going indoors. He has abandoned the area but shows no outward concern or sadness, just resignation, it seems. The day is moving on and it is time to find a new pursuit as Luke has already done.

This next vignette shows the sense of collective interest that the children at Fishergate have in one another's play, as we have also seen to some extent in the vignette above. It's also an example of how flexible and open-ended play materials can allow boys and girls and younger and older children to play together as equally weighted players regardless of the differences in their skills, abilities and interests. Some themes unite them all but this theme has arisen, it seems, from one child quite spontaneously rather than being planned and designed by an adult. It is a good example of what can happen when children have the space, time, experience and resources to get it all together in a familiar environment with familiar peers alongside adults committed to the concept of open-ended play in an early years environment.

In this vignette the children are laying different materials in a line to form a 'walkway' that eventually circumnavigates the playground and joins the end of the 'corridor' that formed part of Archie's and Luke's design (the room itself has disappeared as crates have been removed for the walkway). These physically challenging walkways have been a common feature of different children's outdoor play over the year but none have been as extensive as this one, nor has one involved so many children for such a long period of time – over an hour.

> The walkway begins with the slide, then the yellow plastic shape that Owen was inside earlier, followed by an upside-down crate, then wooden bricks, plastic bricks in a line, a large tyre (a permanent structure with grass inside) and several large plastic water containers on their side. Someone has added shallow crates. Alistair and Roxanna (two five-year-olds) work together to fetch wooden blocks to take the construction around the corner and begin to form a second side. Roxanna seems to be the leader of the play and for a brief period seems to be the sole designer, although Alistair frequently returns to help. Children who are walking on it walk as far as it goes and then return to the beginning. Gradually it gets longer; some are skilful, some are less confident. Some sections require careful balancing. Alistair and Roxanna are clearly cooperating and chatting about the design; they seem to have developed an understanding of common goals. Sadie brings a large red, hard plastic tube but Roxanna pushes it away. Charley (three years old) is anxious about one part of the construction that is wobbly (a large plastic water container), tries to cross it twice, repositions it and then goes around it. Alistair and Roxanna are continuing with wooden blocks and seem intent on using them all. Children wait patiently at the end of the construction for more bricks to be added. Sadie has been trying to talk to Roxanna, who seems not to be interested or does not want interrupting. Sadie pushes over the large red plastic tube (as shown in Figure 2.4) again but Roxanna pushes it away again. Sadie watches Roxanna placing the bricks for a while and then fetches over the orange container with the bricks in so Roxanna does not have to walk so far to get the bricks. Roxanna says nothing but Sadie looks satisfied.
>
> Marco and Stevie (five years) are engaged in some good-natured pushing and smiling as they wait, balanced on the walkway, for the bricks

Figure 2.4 From a 'walkway' to an assault course.

to continue, although Stevie is doing most of the pushing. However, Marco slips and pushes back against Stevie, who takes this as deliberate, pushes hard, announces 'I'm not your friend' and walks away. The other boys seem unconcerned and Marco straightens the bricks. Prior to this, this group of boys have been playing together all morning building ramps and designs for cars; they have a long history as friends. Stevie returns to the beginning of the 'walk' and then joins his waiting friends quietly and smiles at Marco, who returns the smile and they chat about the walkway being broken just behind them. Other children are playing on different parts of the walkway which now has three sides. Melinda tries the walk with her backpack on – she has had it on all morning and since, as one staff member points out, the recent class trip. Some balancing is difficult for her. An adult points out to her that this is because of her backpack and suggests she might take it off but Melinda shakes her head. The walkway has been broken by this point and other children begin to repair it. Someone says to Roxanna 'I don't think this is going to work.' She says 'OK' and walks away from the construction. She looks back once over her shoulder but does not return.

A bigger group of younger children are on it now and Jason, Roxanna, Stevie and Marco have all left. The younger children miss out the bits that are difficult. Gradually the walkway is reconstructed by Julia (aged five years) and older and younger children are in the line together – about 15 of them and the numbers grow. Noah gets his bricks on his arms again and is back to being a robot. The red plastic tube is added to the walkway and Julia announces 'Don't go under this, go over, it's got water in. OK?' The message is passed down the line; one girl does a thumbs-up and smiles. Someone asks 'What happens if we fall?' and someone responds 'It's your fault if you fall.' Someone else: 'Come on everyone.' They walk across builders' sacks, saying 'Come on, come on; you have to go in a line everyone.' Owen has joined in and follows on. There's lots of talking, listening, waiting and watching. They are now on the fourth side and nearly back to the beginning. Julia, still in charge of design, announces 'These are a bit higher, guys, OK?' Pearl (five years): 'Don't worry if you wobble.' Julia says 'Lower. Lower again', telling those in the queue behind her of a height change in the walkway. One girl tries to take a crate from Luke and Archie's corridor and another says 'You'd better not, that's the entrance'; although no one has played in this area for some time she has clearly been aware of its purpose. They have taken the construction to the original corridor although many of the crates from the 'room' have been used. Sebastian, who has poor physical coordination, is climbing on the walkway too, falls off once but climbs on again, rubbing his elbow and looking as if he may cry – but doesn't. He does not join the line of children but seems absorbed in his own world of play, perhaps taking advantage of a construction he is not yet able to produce himself. Archie has come out and looks at what is left of his design for a few moments and then goes indoors again. It's time to get ready for lunch. Pearl looks at the design and says 'We're almost at the start and that's the ending.'

EYFS learning outcomes

PSRN: Use everyday words to describe position.

CLL: Interact with others, negotiating plans and activities and taking turns in conversations. Use language to imagine and recreate roles and experiences.

PD: Move with confidence, imagination and safety.

Reflecting on the play

There is tremendous amount of fluidity in this play, in which at no time does an adult participate. Different members of staff do come outside and observe the play and some take photographs of their key children as they are involved in the play. As Andy and Pat watch the film, Andy remarks that Roxanna, the originator of the idea, has a mother in the army and one can only wonder if she has seen assault courses or heard her mother speak of them and that this is what she has in mind here. Although we had referred to it as a 'walkway' (and do so above in the description of the play) 'assault course' may be a more appropriate term.

Although the originators of the idea leave the play, others seem to see its potential and choose to take it forward – quite literally, creating a finished design that returns to its starting point and spans the breadth and width of the outdoor space. The need for safety warnings is implicit; older children are seen explaining to younger ones and occasionally assisting transition in tricky areas but children are never seen to ask for help. They either master the challenge or go around the risky obstacle quite happily as Charley (three years old) does. These children are being challenged mathematically through the design process and through the selection of appropriate materials, as well as geographically in their intention to use as much space as possible and physically in managing their own bodies. The language is constant as they use praise, questions and instructions and give advice. The younger children are clearly internalising these processes through their own careful observations and occasional imitation as they straighten a wonky part of the course. The levels of collaboration and intellectual challenge are huge, with numerous problems being identified and solved.

When Sadie moved the large plastic tube that Roxanna ignored, she clearly had a purpose in mind that Roxanna could not see, or perhaps Roxanna chose not to use the tube because it had water in it, as Julia later pointed out when she did use it. Perhaps Sadie understood that Roxanna was trying to bring different kinds of challenges into the play as Roxanna designed a construction that was high and low, wide and narrow, wobbly and rigid. Sadie was also the one who took the orange container to Roxanna, who was constantly walking across the playground to get one or two bricks at a time from the container. Only careful observation showed the nature of Sadie's thinking here; these actions might have been lost amidst the business but these decisions seem to be important actions for Sadie and seem to have been informed through observation and reflection on her part. The play seems 'loaded' with intellectual, social and physical challenges and alive with creativity. Different children respond to these aspects in different and similar ways.

Conclusion

The detailed descriptions contained in these three vignettes have tried to show the complexity of the children's thinking, actions and interactions in their changing outdoor space. We talked at the outset of how the team had come to see the quality of the children's engagement in the outdoor area and so to reconsider the need for planned themes or topics. We have seen in these vignettes cooperation between pairs, small groups and large, mixed-age groups arising quite spontaneously and without any direct intervention by adults. However, the older children in the unit have, by this time, been engaging with this open-ended space for over a year; they are growing up with it and growing used to it in the company of adults who are also coming to see its value in new and different ways.

Chapter 3 presents further outdoor vignettes and also looks at indoor play at Fishergate.

Chapter 3

Becoming oneself as a playful being and the growth of identity

Looking outdoors and indoors

Chapter 2 noted Archie and Luke's shared interests in recreating domestic scenarios in their play, revisiting spaces where they engage with their parents and other family members and friends on a regular basis. We reflected on whether Roxanna was stimulated to create the 'assault course' because her mother was in the army. We cannot know what the influences are on the children's play but reflecting on these aspects of just these three open-ended play vignettes should give some impetus to the notion that the 'whatever you want it to be place' offers opportunities for engaging with peers and for developing a sense of self that builds quite explicitly on one's day-to-day experiences with powerful role models within the home, the community and the wider environment.

The framing of identity is a complex part of human development; it comes from our engagements and experiences with others and if these are positive and self-affirming experiences (as was surely the case for all the above children in their play on these occasions) we each begin to develop a coherent self narrative. Erikson (1969) discusses how identity development arises from the gradual construction of inner unity, of self-integration and of an understanding of continuity. As children become older, they develop a reflective self-function and a secure enough sense of self (in the right conditions, of course) to build a capacity for resilience (Fongay 2001; Fongay *et al.* 1994). Identity is also about belonging, as Weeks (1990: 88) notes:

> about what you have in common with some people and what differentiates you from others. At its most basic, it gives you a sense of personal location, the stable core to your individuality. But it's also about your relationships, your complex involvement with others and in the modern world these have become more complex and confusing.

There is no doubt that today's young children exist in a complex and confusing world and that, through their play, they seek to make sense of that world and of how it relates to themselves and of how they relate to others in the wider world. We might then argue that, in restricting children's play opportunities to the themes and ideas of adults, we correspondingly restrict the capacities for their identities to blossom in accord with their own experiences, interests and motivation. The 'whatever you want it to be place' would seem to be a perfect place for aligning personal interests and motivations with positive opportunities for identity development. 'Power limits the possibility of identity' (Weedon 2004: 15); if early years environments limit the possibilities for pursuing personal interests, memories and experiences, they are potentially also limiting the possibilities for strong identity formation and the growth of resilience through playful engagements with peers and adults.

The vignettes in this chapter have been selected to continue this exploration of identity in the company of playful peers. We will explore Sebastian's possible preoccupation with building his play around a 'concrete mixer' and the potential links with his father's work as a builder; we will consider a large group of children playing puppies and kittens, common play themes perhaps, but these children seem to be using a wide range of resources to create not just a home but a neighbourhood, with many homes. We will also look at a group of girls, older five-year-olds who seem to have already developed very coherent self narratives and exercise their identities and their personal power through language, caring, conflict and conflict resolution.

Bearing in mind this starting point of identity, before examining the vignettes and beginning to think more about the use of the outdoor and the indoor areas at Fishergate we want to examine the socio-cultural and bio-cultural theories of play. These have particular resonance with identity because identity is shaped both by biology and by social and cultural experiences (Weedon 2004). However, before this, let us listen to two of the staff reflecting on how they are thinking about the developing play in the early years unit.

In this opening quote, Rachel is reflecting on the preoccupations and explorations that she has observed children engage with, repeatedly, over time, when their environment allows them to do so. As Rachel describes this boy's activities, as part of a discussion about why she thinks the outdoor environment is beneficial, one can almost feel the neural pathways being laid down in his brain as he engages again and again with the physics of movement, forces, resistance and transfer. He is engaged in solitary play here, others in cooperative play, but all of them are using play and the resources to create and develop a self narrative:

> They're repeating their play, which I think is fascinating. The more you watch them, the more you see the way they repeat their play. They can be repeating it but then they're tweaking it slightly. We've got one child, it's absolutely fascinating to watch, and he's been exploring gradients and bridges and other things. Wherever he is, inside or out, he'll play with water or he'll collect bricks and make channels going down and he'll slide things down and he'll put different things inside, like a bowl or he'll put in a wooden block to slow the bowl going down the slope, he'll put something in front of the bowl and I was just sitting and watching it and said 'ooo, ooo' and he was so excited with it and outside he started putting other things

down the steps and looking at the other side of the slide and going down the slide and down the steps and looking at the different way things fall down. They then put their whole bodies down and they made a waterslide and put their bodies down the waterslide and it's just fascinating at how the ideas connect together and how they progress and how they're trying out different things to see if they work.

In her interview with Pat, Jane put it a little differently but, as a relatively new member of staff, she is also showing how she is tuning into the opportunities that children have in this environment to both go and grow with the flow. Jane also sees the importance of the link with family life in terms of identity and intellectual growth:

Jane: I think you have a closer bond with these children because you are knowing them, you're not just knowing how they can work. There's a family environment they have at this school which I've not found anywhere else. Families are welcomed in and you get to know them and their history. Everyone's interested in that; it's not just a case that you've come to school and dropped them off at the door and go.

Pat: So it's partly successful because families feel connected to the school and are welcome, it's partly successful because the children have choices and options to pursue and adults who are interested in helping them make those choices; is it anything to do with the actual resources; for example is that outdoor area familiar to you?

Jane: No, I've never seen anything like it before till I came here. I think it is the full package, I don't think it would work as well if any of those were missing. I've never seen anything like the outdoor area, but straight away I could see how it could work better. My very first encounter I thought 'errr . . . ' but then you start to think 'oh!' You can see why they don't have the usual swings or slides or climbing frames because it's about them using their imagination and making other things out of the resource.

In Rachel's earlier reflection there is no sense of repetition of activity being a conservative or limiting activity for a child or for the peers similarly engaged with him; rather it seems to be a preoccupation with mastery and understanding at a deeply personal and meaningful level. Jane elaborates on this by acknowledging the need to connect with the child within his or her family but extends this by saying that 'connecting with the family' is insufficient of itself. The play environment needs to allow the child to bring family-related experiences from beyond school into school, though their play. Each member of the early years team reveals how their own thinking and understanding of learning processes in a playful learning environment are continuing to grow and develop.

Susan Greenfield (2000: 65) reflects on the relationship between brain development and the influences on the growth of identity when she writes:

> The more complex the brain, the greater the potential for variations in the neuronal connectivity that underlies its interpretations. The longer the childhood, the more the brain will be able to forge connections that mirror not just the demands of the species or the immediate habitat, but the particular and peculiar history of the individual concerned.

Greenfield's reflections are echoed from a somewhat different perspective by Vandenbroeck (1999), who is examining the ways in which young children are exposed to and engage with diversity within their early years environment. He discusses also that the creation of identity is akin to the writing of one's own history and future as the child takes experience and memory and re-engages and reshapes their sense of self in the complex world around them.

In terms of Rachel's reflection and at this point in time, this boy's history is particularly aligned with a set of ideas linked with *the movement of materials* (water/objects) and *connections* (gradients/bridges) and these are being persistently explored – something seen quite a lot in the play of many children captured on film during the research. In terms of his development and perhaps of his survival, it is clearly in his brain's best interests to consolidate and extend these neural pathways at times of optimal growth. His preoccupations then may be not only natural, but perhaps essential to him as a biological being. As Jarvis (2010: 63) points out, also echoing Jane's reflections: 'human beings are clearly a complex mixture of evolved and culturally mediated behaviours' and these biological and cultural dimensions are aspects the book will examine, at various points.

Socio-cultural and bio-cultural theories of play: the mastery of play

Chapter 1 introduced some theoretical frames of reference that drew from the work of Vygotsky and which also referenced the substantial further and more recent developments related to socio-cultural theory; in her work Jarvis (2010) explores the bio-cultural influences relating, in this case, to gendered play. Socio-cultural theory and bio-cultural theory draw from similar roots of understanding, with the bio-cultural debates bringing to the fore the nature–nurture perspectives and the contribution of hormones in determining biological identity. These are complex and wide-ranging debates and there is not space to do them justice here, but in relation to identity we make some passing reference in order to locate bio-culturalism in the frame with socio-cultural perspectives, especially in relation to gendered play, which we will be considering. Andy and Pat's joint reflections on the filmed material included frequent and long ponderings on the distinctions and similarities between boys' and girls' play and we cannot ignore these dimensions when considering identity development through play.

Vygotsky did not view play as 'naturalistic', that is, as an outgrowth of children's instinctive tendencies. He believed play to be a cultural-historical phenomenon largely dependent on the degree and quality of adult mediation and engagement (Bodrova 2008: 359). This would suggest, for example, that the preoccupations and engagements of Archie and Luke in the previous chapter came, not from generally recognised universal play themes, but from their own cultures and histories as four- and five-year-old boys growing up in York in the new millennium. They may have much in common with other children, but equally they may not; we should not assume that all children want to play as they did, although, as we saw from their second vignette, relatively large numbers of children took an active interest in their play and Archie and Luke appeared to have very mixed feelings about that with some children being welcomed and others seemingly not so welcome.

Interestingly, during the period of observation at Fishergate, although we saw other children constructing many kinds of 'spaces to be occupied' outdoors, with tarpaulins, boxes, builders' sacks and the like, no one ever constructed the kinds of spaces that Archie and Luke constructed together and, as far as the filmed record and recollections show, no adults were ever involved in Archie and Luke's home-based designs, although later we will consider a student teacher's involvement in creating a telescope with them. Taking Vygotsky's perspective of play as 'not naturalistic' might lead to an interpretation of Archie and Luke's play as a conceptualisation of familiar environments, a need to intellectually inter-nalise the domestic and public spaces they regularly inhabit. Their play looked very naturalistic and perhaps the key issue relates to how the word 'naturalistic' is defined. Without knowing what Archie's and Luke's homes looked like we might still, legitimately, presume that they are recreating them from memory and therefore their play is being culturally influenced.

Bodrova (2008) goes on to say of Vygotsky's work how it illustrates that play becomes the means by which children develop new forms of thinking. In play, children act in accordance with internal ideas rather than in relation to external realities; but Archie and Luke seem to be combining internal ideas with the external realities of the materials, spaces and time available to them, although we do not know if they hold the same ideas about what they are doing. We can say, because they play together for such long periods, that they have found ways to combine their ideas and their personal realities and also that their play environment and the adults in it allow them to do this on a regular basis and for extended periods of time.

Vygotsky argued that the creation of imaginary play situations could be regarded as the development of abstract thought as children sought to reproduce and re-engage with their own developing conceptual understanding of how the world works and of how they might be proactive within that world. Elkonin (2005) introduced the terms 'mature' or 'advanced' players where object substitutes are regularly used much as we saw also in Archie and Luke's play; related roles become more complex and are substantially language-based, and the 'rules of engagement' are implicitly understood without constant reiteration by the playing children. Reynolds and Jones (1997) talk of 'master players' when older children plan their play through extended and complex negotiations and their play scenarios can continue for several weeks, as key ideas are revisited and extended over time; we explore this further in Chapter 6. They state that: 'In play, young children are constructing their knowledge of the world by representing what they know.' Play is children's 'self-chosen process of recreating experience in order to understand it' (Reynolds and Jones 1997: 3). A key question concerns the extent to which children are allowed/enabled to pursue these 'self-chosen processes' in the average early years setting. Are they allowed to reach the level of master players? Do they get the lengths of uninterrupted time that the children did in the first three vignettes we have studied?

Interconnecting play, culture and identity

This chapter draws from vignettes of play occurring in both the outdoor and indoor areas but we begin with Ashley and Sebastian – the same Sebastian who in the previous chapter (vignette 2) was finding it difficult to understand and participate in the play activities of other children (you may recall, he threw a plank into the 'house' after he had been 'ejected') and who, in the walkway/assault course play (vignette 3), was exhibiting large motor skills that were still in development. Following on from this focus on Ashley and Sebastian, in a search for a better understanding of how play, identity and culture are interconnected, we look at the play of individual children and groups of boys and girls both indoors and outdoors.

Vignette 4

Sebastian and Ashley are both new to the unit and Sebastian has English as a second language. They are playing with the 'red tube' of vignette 3 (as shown in Figure 2.4) in Chapter 2. It stands just over a metre high and is open at both ends. It has a diameter of about half a metre and the open ends are a little narrower than the bulk of the tube. It is almost circular but has ridges all around; it is not a smooth surface, thus making it impossible to roll.

Ashley is 'digging' with a spade in the plastic tube, which he has filled with wooden bricks: 'It's spiders. Spiders' he shouts. Patience comes to him: 'Where?' She looks inside. Ashley shouts to no one in particular 'keep digging'. Then he shouts: 'It's a coal fire, it's a coal fire.' Sebastian has come over and is placing more wooden bricks in the tube as Ashley is 'digging'. Patience is now transporting water to another site (which it later becomes apparent is also a fire). Ashley and Sebastian begin fighting over the spade; Sebastian is trying to pull it away from Ashley and saying 'Mine'. Pat stops filming and explains to Sebastian that there is another spade inside; he goes to get it and returns to the tube. They both have to stand on crates to reach into it with their spades. They both 'dig' in the bricks and lift out bricks and drop them to the floor. Ashley accidentally hits Sebastian on his head with the spade; 'Ow' says Sebastian and rubs at it, looks briefly angry but then gets down to retrieve another brick and replace it in the tube. Ashley moves away and Sebastian pushes at the tube until it falls on its side. He starts to roll it but it gets stopped by indentations on the side. He begins to pull out bricks. Ashley returns and replaces them. Ashley tries to roll the tube. Sebastian comes to help push and they attempt to push it together. Ashley begins to pile up the bricks just away from the tube. Sebastian is examining the tube as if trying to work out why it will not roll. He then gives a brick to Ashley, who places it on the pile. They build together fetching bricks from inside the tube. Sebastian looks at the brick construction and then pushes it over; they begin again. Sebastian is building a tower as before but Ashley is now putting the bricks in a straight line along the floor. Sebastian comes to help him and then removes bricks from his tower to give to Ashley. Ashley adds more bricks to the line. Sebastian piles them up for him to use. Ashley allows him to take more bricks. Patience appears and throws water into the red tube, still perhaps pursuing a fire theme. Sebastian and Ashley are building a tower together. It falls and they both laugh and scream together. Paul comes across (from the fire he is making with Patience) and takes the spade, which has been on the floor for some time. Ashley goes to him and snatches it back. Paul says: 'I want it.' Ashley replies: 'Can't have it.' They both pull at it and look to Pat in mute supplication to get it sorted for them. Pat explains to Paul that Ashley is still playing with it and had just put it down for a little while. Paul accepts this and goes away. Sebastian and Ashley continue to build towers. Sebastian lays the bricks in a line on their side – a new arrangement. Ashley is 'digging' again in the tube, which he has placed upright again; he goes over to the tap and returns. Sebastian has a long line of bricks on which he carefully walks. Ashley copies this. Sebastian kicks the bricks away and then starts adding them to the far side of the line of bricks. He arranges two bricks end to end and lines them up carefully. He stands one brick on end. He makes a pile of four bricks, lifts them and throws them in another tray. Sebastian tries to take a green jug from Patience as she passes and the student teacher says that Patience is still playing with it. Sebastian goes over to the water tap and tries again. Patience resists him. Paul has managed to get hold of a spade and is 'shovelling' the other fire that Patience is putting out with her water. Sebastian gets a paint pot to carry water and throws it in the tube. He tries again to get Patience's green jug. Pat takes him inside and they find a white jug that makes him smile. He runs out to fill it and then goes to the outdoor water tray and watches his water run down the ramp. He repeats this several times, watching the water carefully. He pours water down the grate and tries to lift it. He pours water down the guttering attached to the wall and then returns to the water tray to continue his play there.

EYFS learning outcomes

PSE: Have a developed awareness of their own needs and feelings and can be sensitive to the needs, views and feelings of others.

PSRN: Use and develop mathematical ideas and methods to solve practical problems.

CD: Use their imagination in art and design, music, dance, imaginative and role play and stories.

Both Andy and Rachel subsequently noted that Sebastian returned to this water play the following day; Rachel also remarked that he had played in the water area the previous day. On the day following this vignette, Sebastian had also asked Rachel for the red tube and for bricks to pile in it, replicating the previous day's play but without Ashley. He then played alone for about 20 minutes similarly to the day before with the red tube on its side for some of the time and upright for other periods of time. We can see that, for Sebastian, there is an inter-connection of play interests, a continuity of immersion in particular ideas and explorations, and very clearly a strong sense of memory and recall relating to what is interesting and satisfying for him.

As we watched the film of this play, Andy and Pat tried to understand the meanings that the children were making and recorded the following reflections:

The first play theme that seems evident is a fire theme from Ashley, and Sebastian seems content to engage with this for a while. However, as Sebastian pushes the container of bricks over he seems to have another idea going. Although they're not talking to one another they are interested enough in one another to watch one another. Ashley wants the container to be returned to the upright position, doesn't he? They aren't communicating through language but they are watching one another. They seem to be searching for ways of connecting with one another. Patience is putting water on the bricks, the fire; this is the first time she has done this. What this shows is that in the right environment with the right materials it may not matter if they aren't yet using language. Unless you were watching these two boys closely, you wouldn't understand the extent of the connection that is going on here.

The spades are really important to them and when adults say 'you have to share' what they don't seem to realise is they are changing the play and removing something important in the development of the emerging or established play themes. Other children can understand that once it's explained to them far more than adults can, it seems, as Paul accepted the explanation but did not lose sight of his desire to have a spade and succeeded later. Just a few months ago when Patience was new, she was crying and often seemed distressed. Now she is in command, knows where everything is and is helping other children as well as hanging on to objects she doesn't want to lose. She resists Sebastian well and is learning to be assertive.

Even when Ashley and Sebastian argue, they seem to want to stay together either because they both want access to these materials or because they like being together or perhaps both. This might be the forming a closer relationship with one another, perhaps the beginning of friendship; at the least, a realisation that others have interests similar to one's own.

Sebastian's balancing on the bricks seems to be linked with a determination to master the skill of balancing, which is still not a comfortable part of his physical repertoire.

Paul and Patience are playing intensively and extensively at the management of a life-threatening situation – the fire. Each of these tasks is about the development of competence in a world where these skills are essential to them.

When Sebastian received the white jug, did it remind him of the activities he had been engaged in the day before in the water tray – activities that Rachel had subsequently recognised as significant and ongoing for him? Was a pleasant memory reactivated for him? Is this why he smiled?

Knowing Sebastian's home life well, Andy had a sudden revelation and said: 'I think what Sebastian is doing is being a builder. His dad is a builder and he has been into the unit to build a wall for us. I bet Sebastian has seen him do these things at home. I think he turns the tube over because it's a cement mixer and he puts water in for that reason, not because of the fire. That's Ashley's and Patience's theme but Sebastian's I think is a cement mixer.'

Some months later, Andy observed Sebastian and other boys mixing earth and water to make mud. After several days, this progressed to wall-building as they used the mud to add house bricks to an existing wall; this play seemed to emerge from the boys' conversations without any adult direction and as they played they demonstrated that they understood the technical demands of wall-building. This may have come from memories of Sebastian's father building the wall in their early years unit or from demonstrations from individual children (Sebastian) or from both influences. From somewhere they had learned or were learning some principles of wall-building as a skilled enterprise. At this later point in time, perhaps recalling the earlier conversations about Sebastian's father being a builder, Andy also remarked on a good friendship that had developed between Sebastian and Dom. Dom's father was an architect; this could of course be coincidence – the son of a builder and the son of an architect forming a friendship – or it could reflect recognition of shared interests by the boys, over time, born of their respective cultural and perhaps genetic heritages.

Friendships, power, sites and objects: personalising play

Having noted Sebastian's difficulties in making relationships and friendships with the other children in vignette 2 in the previous chapter (Archie and Luke's second construction, where he 'invaded' the play and threw a plank into the play site), it might have seemed that there was an important role for the adult in facilitating Sebastian's successful entry to group play at a more general level. However, what also needs to be considered is that, whilst other children may have accepted Sebastian when an adult is present, there is no guarantee the acceptance is replicated when the adult is elsewhere, nor that friendships or relationships can emerge only from proximity. At the time of vignette 2, Sebastian was not displaying the skills of successful play entry and interaction and he was still developing his English language skills but it would seem, given his subsequent abilities to make and keep friends, that both these necessary areas of skill acquisition were in development through Sebastian's own efforts and activities in this open-ended play environment. In vignette 4 above, which took place two months before vignette 2, and also when Sebastian was very new to the unit, Sebastian was displaying a capacity for both communication and peer engagement in activities that the players had themed and sustained without any adult intervention other than to make the materials and time available to the children and to let them get on with it. Sebastian shows that he can sustain an interactive proximity to others when his own play theme is to the fore (vignette 4) and can demonstrate achievement of the EYFS learning outcomes through cooperative play. Perhaps he has not yet learned to understand that other children's narratives are to the fore when they design the play (vignette 2) and that he must negotiate access; however, this capacity does come a little later in time, as we see in Chapter 6.

In vignette 4, the open-ended materials and the flexible play environment had given Sebastian the chance to achieve what an adult's direct intervention might or might not have been successful in supporting. However, in addition, in vignette 4, Sebastian is engaging with a play activity in which he has determined the play theme and its development, and this seems to be a theme in which his own identity and culture may well be finding 'voice' and 'place'. In this space, at this time, Sebastian feels powerful because he is able to express his inner thoughts and experiences and from this feeling of power stems a desire and the opportunity to develop stronger links with a similarly engaged peer. When we compare Sebastian's play engagement in vignette 4 with an apparently less successful engagement that occurred two months after this, we can see how wrong it would be to base a judgement of Sebastian's skills and engagement levels on the later episode only (vignette 2); we can see also perhaps how *personalised context* and *meaning-making* play a significant part in skill display and that to have judged Sebastian's skills only on an episode that came two months later (when we might also have presumed he was 'further developed') would have resulted in a serious undermining of his actual potential and skills.

Although playing at 'fires' in vignette 4, Patience's other big interest, which comes across in many of the filmed extracts and the observational notes, is that of 'magic potions'. It spans both her indoor and outdoor play over several months and is a theme that emerged in other children's play too, particularly the younger children in the unit. Not all children seem to play at potions but some children do seem to play repeatedly at it. Sometimes it happens on a big scale with several children playing together around a water tray, for example, into which they have placed soil, leaves, sticks, glitter, pine cones and so on (Figure 3.1).

Although the potions are mixed in one place, the filling of smaller containers allows the play to be more mobile and also to be undemandingly sociable for those children who have not yet established the kind of friendships that were very evident across the five-year-olds in the unit who had known one another for a long period – and who seldom, if ever, played at magic potions. Both boys and girls played at potions, often in mixed gender groups.

Within the stories with which these children are becoming familiar, magic potions of course are very powerful concepts. They give the children a sense of powerfulness equivalent to that of superheroes (Marsh 1999, 2000), an inherent capacity to rise above day-to-day life and to be something out of the ordinary. The magic potion, just as with being a superhero, brings a new dimension of possibility to life and so impinges on one's sense of identity and of self.

Figure 3.1 Potions being mixed.

Magic potions and superheroes are cultural artefacts; indeed, in the present day, they represent substantial commercial incomes within the media and, as a consequence, children have constant exposure to them. These children are surrounded by these images and possibilities; they are culturally familiar and comfortable and so invade their day-to-day lives when the possibility for them to do so arises. They then become opportunities for shared meaning-making with relatively unfamiliar children as they come to recognise similar interests and purpose – just as Ashley and Sebastian did in an encounter as new children and as Archie and Luke have done, over time. It seems that, when children identify themes, objects and possibilities that can connect them in undemanding ways with other children, they are ready to exploit the possibilities if the environment will let them.

Looking at the indoor area

This chapter and the previous chapter have explored in some detail the development of the outdoor area into a more creative space and the ways in which this seemed to be impacting positively on the daily lives of the children and the adults. It might be informative at this stage to explore the processes which led to similar developments to the indoor areas, brought about by an early years team which had observed the powerful effect that the use of open-ended materials was having on the children.

Elizabeth, who had worked in the unit full-time for four years, identified some distinctions between the outdoor and indoor areas when she had been reflecting on changes within the unit during her time there. It might be recalled from previous chapters that the initial impetus for change had come from a desire to develop the outdoor area. Andy had commented previously that the indoor and outdoor spaces had seemed too similar, the outdoors merely being an extension of the indoors, and that they had thought about what they might do to address this. As a consequence of parental contribution of materials and the children's initiative-taking, the outdoor space had begun to take on a new look and a new feel and Elizabeth, reflecting with hindsight, commented:

> I think they're a lot more adventurous outside. They . . . it's hard to explain really, inside it looks a bit more structured . . . but outside I think they've got more challenges. You can see their minds working, trying to work it out, and solving their problems. Inside it's more . . . there's a writing area and it's there for you but outside they make and solve their own problems, in whatever they're building or doing.

Inevitably, the spaces will look different not least because of their geography and the kinds of materials available; however, the indoor area was also subject to reflection and development by the staff team.

These developments began with reflections that members of the early years team made about keeping the learning journey books and, in this section, Andy has written about the developments over time. These books were the records of the observations and achievements of the children kept by the staff for each of their key children. After the developments in the outdoors, the learning journey books filled rapidly with notes, photographs, quotations of the children talking about their play, and staff analysis. Members of staff noted that there were far more observations and photographs of the children's play in the outdoor area and were intrigued to find out why that would be. As Andy recalled:

> We analysed this as a team and came to the conclusion that, for lots of reasons, the staff were more drawn to observe the children's play in the outdoor area. This seemed to be mainly because of the unpredictability and challenge of it all. Observing and making sense of what we were seeing on a day-to-day basis was a big challenge for the adults and led us all to become intrigued and keen to capture and record what we could.

The play had so few adult directives and was so influenced by play themes introduced by the children, as we have seen in the vignettes so far, that it had become as absorbing for the adults to watch and capture as it was for the children to be involved. What, though, did this say about the indoor spaces? Was the play of less value to the children if it was less fascinating for the adults or did this simpler, more easily explained and defined play meet the same needs of the children but in a different way? These were all questions that were explored by members of the early years team.

There were children who seemed to enjoy the added structure of the indoor spaces, but it was also observed that these more prescriptive spaces, such as the home corner kitchen, were accessed mainly by children who were new to the setting and who perhaps took comfort from familiar concepts. Children who had more experience of the setting were often seen to begin their play within the confines of a recognisable structure (the home corner, role play area) but as their ideas developed, their play would become much more mobile, moving within different indoor and outdoor spaces, picking up and discarding objects of play as they went. As Andy reflects:

> We were aware that any developments to the indoor area needed to respect the needs of both the experienced and less experienced players.

The indoor area began to be developed, but not with any clear action plan or goal in mind. It evolved over time as the early years staff discussed and analysed the effects of the outdoor play. One of the first areas for discussion and development was role play. In previous years areas of the classroom had been developed and enhanced by the staff to fit particular topics. These topics would last for half a term at a time. Enhancements were made so that children could explore concepts relating to the topic through their play. In this way, during a vehicles topic, a role play area alongside the home corner would be developed into a garage and a variety of different types of vehicles would be added to the sand and water. As staff in the early years began to move away from this form of planning, questions remained about how areas of provision would continue to be resourced, organised and enhanced. A role play area which remained predetermined as a garage area or shop would seem to be at odds with the form of planning which was emerging whereby observations made by the staff were analysed and then developed into ideas and enhancement for the next day. Reflecting the interests and needs of the children became the main motivation in the development of the indoor areas of provision.

After much discussion, this existing and adult-initiated role play area began to evolve into something rather different. Observations of many of the children creating their own special spaces to play in led to the first development of this area. It included a den area where a large piece of army camouflage netting suspended from the walls on strings enabled the children to have a private space for discussion, planning and play (Figure 3.2). This concept of creating a space for children to do with it what they wanted led Andy to recall the 'whatever you want it to be place' in the previous research undertaken with Pat some years before.

Figure 3.2 The netting is used to create a den.

Andy recalls:

> There were very clear similarities. It was amazing that something so simple as giving the children their own area to do with what they wanted could have such a profound effect on the play that we observed. This den space would start off at the beginning of each day as just an empty space with a camouflage cover over it. As the children's play developed they would collect a whole range of resources from around the room and bring them along to the den. They brought dinosaurs, cars, teacups, plates, play food, mark-making resources and pieces of material. When we saw that themes continued over many days or weeks, we added in resources to support the play. Non-fiction books on dinosaurs and dinosaur posters meant that children had a point of reference for their play. As we had seen with the outdoor area, their play reached a new level in terms of how involved and absorbed in the play the children were.

This area continued to develop over the following years. The areas which seemed to work best within the room, the staff recall, were those which were defined enough for all adults to understand the space, but open-ended in nature so that the children's play was unrestricted. In this way, the den area was developed into a stage area by adding stage blocks and material (Figure 3.3). This space continued to be used by the children in the same way, with resources brought to the space from the surrounding areas. From this play, simple performances would often emerge, with the children collecting chairs from around the room for the audience to sit on and making tickets and posters.

A key part of the previous form of topic-led planning had been the production of children's work in order to display in the classroom and the wider school. In this way, a topic about 'ourselves' might lead to self portraits, finger printing and drawings of our family and friends. The play that staff now observed in both the indoor and outdoor areas was beginning to lead them to question this way of working. This more child-initiated way of working had a very clear effect on the children on a daily basis but it produced far fewer pieces of art work for display. In addition to this, with so many different themes emerging at any one time, children's pictures and paintings could not be displayed together in the way that staff had previously done. What the staff needed was a way of displaying and celebrating the wide range of activities that the children were now engaged in.

The team began to use what were subsequently called 'our gallery walls' (Figure 3.4). These were large display boards backed with coloured paper and covered with a clear plastic backing. This meant that whatever emerged from the children's play could be displayed almost immediately. The boards became

Figure 3.3 'The stage awaits the players.'

Figure 3.4 Our gallery.

a montage of all sorts of different items: photos, models, drawings, writing and paintings. The team also became aware of just how rich and valuable the children's language was in all of this. They noted some of the things that the children said and celebrated their comments on printed banners which were suspended across the room. One said 'we're going on an adventure . . . and this is what is happening.'

The outdoor play was changing and, although the indoor environment might not have the range and type of resources that were now available outdoors, the children's indoor play was also changing, as this chapter, and to some extent the next chapter, aim to illustrate. The next chapter also talks in further detail about the planning process and how this changed at Fishergate over time, but first of all let us look at two more indoor vignettes that show the extent to which these older children have come to manipulate the indoor play area for their own interests and activities.

Vignette 5 offers a description of play alongside children's reflections as they watched the film and Andy and Pat's reflections on the play as they watched it later. This play continued over much of the day so it is only possible to recreate snippets of it here. On first viewing, and indeed when filming the play, it seems quite 'low-level'. When reading the following narrative, there seems to be nothing remarkable here; one might even imagine a fairly experienced educator deeming this play to be 'chaotic', 'without structure' or 'poorly structured';

as Elizabeth had noted, the problem-solving does not seem as evident indoors as outdoors. However, we would argue that a great deal of subtlety is being expressed in the relationships between the children and clear goal orientation. There is a familiarity between peers that brings an associated capacity for recognising skills and abilities in peers, and there is also, we would argue, a significant level of meaning-making that might elude adult observers but that creates a warp and weft of relationship-building across peers using objects, language, culture and identity.

Vignette 5

The narrative of the filming	Children's comments whilst watching the film	Andy's and Pat's reflections
Morning: Edward and Lucy are taking money from the home corner. Much laughter and eye contact as they take it to a small space between the wall and the sofa and hide there for a while. Lucy finds some chopsticks and takes them into the construction area with her and uses them to mix medicine in a bottle. Maisie has started in the home corner but moves into the construction area and begins to manipulate some large plastic construction pieces. Sadie joins Rosie and they talk together about what there are building. They are trying to move the heavy plastic boxes (big enough to climb into) but decide to leave them where they are and begin to climb inside.		This play begins simply but then grows, develops and becomes more complex as time goes on with about seven children interactively involved with the theme at one point. Andy comments that children always take off their shoes and socks for this type of play and did so in his previous class. He does not know why; he has never asked them to do so. It seems to be something they decide for themselves often at an early point in the play. Perhaps they have been hurt previously.

One child is trying to get the chopsticks off Lucy but she hangs on to them laughing, explains why she needs to keep them. Edward goes into the construction area and asks 'what are you doing'? Five players are together now as Lucy joins the group and she and Edward laugh as Edward places a plastic container on her head. The language is full of directions and explanations as they start to build a narrative.

Rosie begins another design with wooden bricks and Edward watches. Edward goes to the fabric box with Lucy and digs to the bottom to select one particular piece, which he takes back to the new construction for covering up. 'Night night' and 'getting to bed and staying there' are emerging themes as is covering and being contained within the bounda- ries of the constructions. Cardboard boxes are found and become kennels with much crawling inside and conversations. The children are now playing in about five sites in the area, all boundaried in some way and created from different materials. Mornings and

Pat asks them if this is one house or lots of houses and Lucy says: 'It's lots of ken- nels for the puppies.' Edward says: 'But I am a kitten.'

Edward announ- ces as he watches: I'm saying 'wear it'. We're getting more blankets; that's for me and Lucy.'

'Rosie's getting more bricks.'

The children talk a lot to one another as they watch the film and often say 'Shall we play at that again?' as if plan- ning the future and knowing that the opportunities will be there for them to do so.

Edward says as he watches: 'I'm holding the tube.' Then he says to his

These children are familiar enough with one another to use and under- stand teasing and humour and it seems an important part of their interactions here. It alternates quite naturally with decision- making in a mature way.

The children are making spaces into enclosures where narratives can unfold and give a focal point for a dramatic enactment. These older children seem famil- iar with the types of enact- ments ongoing around them and tune into and connect with those with which they are interested. They show a capacity to hold onto multiple aspects of focus as they play across the emerging groups and pairs.

The number of sites seems to reflect a con- ceptual engagement with 'street' or 'community'. This is more evident than was the case in Archie's and Luke's enclosure play but these children are night times are features, using the fabric as blankets. The play has continued over most of the morning and continues again in the afternoon with the same players.

Afternoon: Sadie has stood a cardboard box on its end, making it tall; she fetches scissors and begins to make a 'doorway' as agreed in discussion. Edward says: 'I'll do it.' Sadie: 'No, I'll do it, I'm stronger.' This is quite difficult and takes some time but Sadie persists and then they all enter and leave by the doorway several times. They ask for sellotape and continue to enter the box, stand in it and look at the entrance they have made. Edward looks at the hole that has been cut and then moves off to other play in the area; he returns later and helps Sadie to make a door from the piece of card she has previously cut away.

friend: 'We ran back, didn't we?' 'You are in there, Rosie, and Lucy is in there.'

Sadie: 'We made a hole so we could get out; we're going into the kennel.'

older than Archie and Luke and may have better conceptualisations of 'neighbourhood' at this stage in their lives and thus want to replicate it.

Sadie was the girl in vignette 3 (the assault course) who brought new resources to the activity. Here, the 'doorway' is more sophisticated than that of the 'moving crate' that the younger children in previous observations were using. Both served a purpose but here she seems to have a strong sense of design and function.

EYFS learning outcomes

CLL: Sustain attentive listening; respond to what they have heard with relevant comments, questions or actions.

CLL: Use talk to organise, sequence and clarify thinking, ideas, feelings and events.

KUW: Select the tools and techniques they need to shape, assemble and join what they are using.

This group of older children play together quite frequently, and they often revisit similar versions of this 'collective living'. They clearly have shared understandings of how the play can develop and this seems to make them confident, and perhaps feel powerful too: in command of their environment and the materials and objects they encounter in that environment, able to use them to fulfil their shared goals and purposes. There are instances of good-natured teasing and humour that are quite mature and clearly reciprocal. Their conversations are peppered with the giving and accepting of instructions, the sharing of ideas and possibilities for play development and joint problem-setting and solving. They appear to be 'master players' and their play together is effortless and so it looks, on the surface, to be simple and undemanding. However, this simplicity belies a fluidity born of friendship, reciprocity, trust and shared understandings that have developed over time and that are now a part of who they are and what they can do to control and shape their self-made play spaces and the world around them.

We want to pick up and further develop this notion of 'not looking like much but actually being quite complex' in the next vignette. Unlike the mixed gender activities of vignette 5, vignette 6 involves five girls. As with the above group, these girls have known one another for well over a year; they are amongst the oldest children in the unit. They have well-developed personalities with distinctive personal preferences and interests; prior to this there are examples of them playing together in more domestic scenarios, creating and inhabiting spaces together, always vocal and sometimes arguing and disagreeing; language is in constant use in their interactions and we should acknowledge the inherent complexity of keeping discussions and engagement going across a large group.

In the following vignette, the five girls are interactively engaging on two levels of emotional exploration:

- They are discussing how to care for their plastic lizards, which are kept in water and change colour.
- They are confronting, extending and resolving conflicts that arise as they play and that relate to the reality of their own strong desires, feelings and expressions of power.

Just as with the children in vignette 5, they achieve this without any direct intervention from an adult as they play and engage and simultaneously confront and resolve conflict.

Vignette 6

Five girls are walking around as a group indoors, having been outside for a while. Lucy and Pearl have the plastic lizards and the others are watching them. Lucy dangles the lizard at Cassie and they both laugh but Cassie also recoils a little. They gather around a table, a couple sit on chairs, others lean on the table and they chat for a short time about the lizards. Mia gets out a peg board and two of the girls do the same. Lucy is still stroking her lizard and Cassie is beside her, watching her closely. Lucy asks Tina 'When is this lizard's birthday?' Tina replies 'After Christmas' and then says to Pearl 'Yours is after Christmas as well' (referring to her lizard). Tina then says ''Cos they're a family' and smiles at Pearl, who looks thoughtful and then smiles back. Pearl gets her lizard out of the water again. Tina comes round to 'feed' it with the plastic spoon she is carrying and conversation continues. Mia is still playing with the peg board. Cassie gets a peg board and some pegs and says something inaudible to Mia, across the table. Mia looks at Cassie, says in a very angry voice 'I'm not Cassie, you are' and glares at Cassie. Cassie throws her pegs back in the big container and Mia looks across at her.

Pearl, Tina and Lucy are absorbed with the lizards; Cassie moves around the table to sit beside Mia. She pulls the peg container to herself, looks at Mia and announces: 'I'm having all these.' Mia exclaims 'That's not fair' and begins to put some pegs in a smaller bowl. Cassie immediately replies 'You can't have all that.' They each begin to scoop up what they can to fill their smaller bowls. Mia shouts 'Where's yours, you've got them all.' Cassie counts groups of pegs loudly, 'One, two, three, four, five', and pulls a face at no one in particular. Pearl has looked up from her lizard at Cassie and says quietly to her that she has got more than five but Cassie says she hasn't (angrily); Mia says she has (angrily). Pearl says 'Let me count' and leans across the table to count the pegs and 'prove' there are more than five. She just looks at Cassie when she has finished count-ing, her look seeming to say 'I told you so'.

Lucy is playing with her lizard: 'Oh it's getting cold in here' in a 'lizard-voice'. Pearl responds and they continue their lizard play. Cassie is count-ing her pegs more carefully and Mia is still scooping pegs and looking angrily at Cassie. Cassie announces 'That's not 10 that's none' and reaches for more pegs. Mia throws her pegs down and pulls a 'crying' face, moving a little to stand beside Pearl; she aims her 'crying face' at Pearl, who does not seem to notice. Tina has left the play by this time; Pearl seems to be attempting to ignore Mia to carry on the lizard play but Mia makes louder crying noises and turns to face Pearl. Mia then turns and shouts angrily at Cassie 'Cassie, that wasn't very nice' and Cassie pulls a 'do I look as if I care' face and says: 'I'll tell my dad, you don't even know my dad.' Mia responds but seems less angry and begins putting her pegs back in the large container. Cassie is arranging pegs in the peg board; Mia says something quietly but firmly to Cassie and puts her hands on her hips, moving the upper half of her body towards her. Cassie wipes her nose on her sleeve and puts her tongue out. Mia leans angrily towards her again with her hands still on her hips and says something inaudible quietly but angrily. She then sits down, holding out a peg to Cassie. As Cassie goes to take it, Mia snatches it back and Cassie almost smiles. Mia is still angry but begins putting pegs in her own board. Pearl and Lucy are playing with their lizards. Cassie and Mia watch them. Mia holds her hands out to Pearl, who places the lizard gently on them; after a while Pearl takes it back and continues to play with Lucy. Mia leaves the table and goes to Tina, who is playing elsewhere, and the other girls follow her.

It feels that what is happening here is far too subtle and mature for EYFS referencing so we will move on to the subsequent reflections.

Andy and Pat reflected as follows as they watched the film:

At one point Andy smiled and remarked that Cassie almost seemed to be deliberately 'winding Mia up' as if she wanted the altercation to escalate; the movement to sit beside Mia seemed to mark the beginning of its escalation. Cassie seemed intent on creating a conflict scenario that she felt comfort-able with but Mia, although seemingly angry and overwhelmed to begin with, gradually regained control enough to tease Cassie when she snatched the peg away; and Cassie's half-smile suggested that she saw the humour in this. Cassie's facial expressions were a key part of her personality; she is already assertive and confident and seems almost to be practising the power of 'the look'; she seemed to have a well-developed understanding of the potential power of facial expressions within conflict situations.

Lucy completely ignored the altercation being deeply immersed in care for her lizard, whereas Pearl made an attempt to be the rational peacemaker; a role captured elsewhere on film. Pearl seems to understand the importance of appropriate intervention in conflict; she is careful not to take sides here but to point out to Cassie that she is deliberately miscounting her pegs. Pearl does this calmly and without threat to Cassie; her whole demeanour remains relaxed; she then expresses slight impatience at Mia when she tries to draw Pearl back into the altercation a little later on with her 'crying face'. Pearl seems quite happy to ignore it and seems to recognise this is not real 'upset'.

We considered that Cassie and Mia might be unconsciously or part-consciously colluding in trying to get Lucy and Pearl away from their absorption with the lizards and, in recognising that they were not going to be successful, returned to a state of friendship. The anger and antagonism looked real but yet seemed contained and controlled by Cassie, Pearl and Mia.

Because of the way the day is structured in indoor and outdoor areas the unit, the children have extended periods of time to fully engage with one another in their selected activities; in this vignette, the pegs and the lizards had different levels of status. The lizards were important artefacts around which caring scenarios were being built. The pegs 'just happened to be there' but seemed to serve as useful props in a serious yet playful engagement with conflict and

Table 0.1 Playful pedagogies and playful learning: the juxtaposition model

'Open-ended play': understanding playful pedagogies	'The whatever you want it to be place': revealing playful learning
A way for the adult to conceive of her/ his own role in creating and sustaining an educational environment that is flexible enough to allow children's interests and experiences to emerge and develop; it also encompasses the adults' responsibilities in identifying, recording and planning for those interests in systematic but flexible ways and a responsibility to look for ways of extending those interests and relating them to the wider world in which the child is living and learning. The early years setting becomes a space and place where adults nurture potential and push the boundaries of their personal understandings of playful learning and playful pedagogies.	The environment and its possibilities as perceived and engaged with from the child's perspective. The child enters a space where anything is possible – whether a large or small space – and where they can engage alone or with others in exploring and exploiting that environment to match the images, plans and memories that emerge from their own minds, experiences and skills. The early years setting becomes a space and place where children explore their identity, potential and interests and push back the boundaries of personal possibility through playful engagement.

conflict resolution, an essential skill in human engagement and something that is looked at in greater depth in Chapter 5.

Let us remind ourselves at this point of the teaching–learning model that was introduced in Chapter 1 and around which the book is aiming to structure this exploration of playful learning and playful pedagogies (Table 0.1).

The vignettes explored thus far, both outdoors and indoors, have focussed most substantially on examining the right hand side of the model – the 'whatever you want it to be place' – by seeking to examine the play from the children's perspectives. Chapter 4 goes on to look in more detail at the adult's role in supporting playful pedagogies – to focus a little more substantially on the left hand side of the model whilst also looking for opportunities to continue to shed some light on the right hand side.

Chapter 4

Participating in playful pedagogies

Adults as creative planners and players

The previous chapters have explained how the new ways of working are evolving at Fishergate over time. So far, we have focussed on vignettes that involve children playing with their peers. By studying the children as they coengage in these self-selected, shared spaces we begin to gain more explicit insights into their playful learning and into how children turn open-ended spaces into places where they can be 'whatever they want to be'; to purposefully engage with their own experiences and memories. The vignettes have allowed us to illustrate and explore how the children's play themes and preoccupations are connected with their wider cultural experiences from within and outside school, and also how they are linked with their own emerging sense of individuality, personality and interests. We have seen that these interests are sustained by the children, through their play, over days and weeks if observers are able to discern this and if materials are available to facilitate this.

It has also been noted how, to the 'untrained' eye, their play may seem low-level and without challenge at times, but we have argued that, on the contrary, we are seeing expert or master players at work: 'teams' or pairs of players who have, over time, become familiar with the narratives and preoccupations in which their peers have an interest and with which, through the development of close relationships and friendships, they have chosen to engage because they are recognised as inter-connecting with their own themes and interests. This is by no means the random selection of parallel players or the chance engagement with a passing peer, but rather the active seeking out and commitment to peers with common thematic and intellectual interests as individual children strive to make meaning in the complicated and challenging world around them and, as they build friendships with their peers.

Chapter 5 looks at issues around risk and conflict in play and Chapter 6 examines some age-related distinctions in the children's play, to show the flow from new, solitary player to friendship-based play. However, first of all, it seems timely to look more closely at the role of and challenges for the adult as a playful pedagogue, as addressed on the left of the model around which this book is framed (Table 4.1).

Previous chapters have shown how the children are engaging in the complicated business of making meaning in their lives, through their play and in

Table 4.1 Left hand side of the juxtaposition model

'Open-ended play': understanding playful pedagogies
A way for the adult to conceive of her/his own role in creating and sustaining an educational environment that is flexible enough to allow children's interests and experiences to emerge and develop; it also encompasses the adults' responsibilities in identifying, recording and planning for those interests in systematic but flexible ways and a responsibility to look for ways of extending those interests and relating them to the wider world in which the child is living and learning.
The early years setting becomes a space and place where adults nurture potential and push the boundaries of their personal understandings of playful learning and playful pedagogies.

an open-ended play environment that one child has named 'the whatever you want it to be place'. This chapter looks at how adults might begin to make sense of it all in their busy daily lives in classrooms, and, preoccupied as they must inevitably become, with the vast array of accountability procedures that have surrounded and perhaps, at times, engulfed them. The next section takes a brief look at some of those policy requirements.

Requirements for assessing children's learning in the Foundation Stage

Leading on from the introduction of the EYFS was a clear requirement to observe and record children's learning in keeping with the Assessment and Reporting Arrangements. The EYFS Foundation Stage Profile document (QCA 2003) detailed the early learning goals for children to have achieved by the end of the Foundation Stage. At this point the teacher completes a computer-based assessment for each child towards the end of their reception year. From May 2008, local authorities had a statutory duty to 'monitor and moderate the EYFS profile judgements to ensure that providers are making assessments that are consistent across settings' (*Statutory Framework for the Early Years Foundation Stage* 2007: 17). These records have then been returned to the Local Authority for compiling into an overall record of achievement for a cohort of reception children, in effect becoming a means of measuring the efficacy of the provision against the targets. These would be available to Ofsted inspectors in any subsequent inspection of the school and schools would also be able to compare their own 'scores' with an average for the city or area in which they were located.

Within the assessment requirements were 117 targets across the six areas of provision in the EYFS (DfES 2007), constituting 13 scales, each with nine assessment points and requiring an evidenced measurement for each child. Teams of moderators from the Local Authority would visit the school and all 13 scales would be moderated, over a two- or three-year cycle, using evidence provided by the early years team or reception teacher. The collection and storage of this evidence became a substantial task and could assume a level of importance that overshadowed the use of observation for the identification of children's interests and passions as expressed in their play. We can see how it could lead towards the creation of teacher-directed tasks designed to allow the teacher to collect specific pieces of evidence and how these too might create a curricular experience that would overshadow children's choices.

As was discovered with the Year 6 SATS, having a small number of children with some degree of developmental delay in the class could substantially shift the overall outcome for the class as a whole. However, what must be borne in mind here is that these assessments and measurements are concerned with five-year-olds who might have, within normal measures of development, some apparent developmental delay when 'tested' in such a summative fashion at such an early stage in their lives. In these cases, children were being assessed in contexts which took no account of social and cultural influences on learning and no account of children's abilities to influence one another's learning (Carr *et al.* 2005), as previous vignettes have amply illustrated that they are capable. Neither of course does it take any account of children's inherent abilities, once encouraged to do so, to make their own judgements about their own activities (Brooker 2008; Claxton 1995). As Brooker (2008: 129) notes: 'children's growing involvement in activities, their growing sense of belonging to the group, and their growing contributions to the group culture are the significant signs of learning'.

What Brooker describes is much more challenging to measure than a requirement to tick summative, outcomes-related boxes. Building these kinds of measures into assessment policy carries an inherent requirement to trust educators, and also of course to educate them in developing the ability to monitor development over time, rather than 'in the moment'. An emphasis on recording summative assessments, against narrow indicators, at a given point in time, also, we would argue, acts to diminish the likelihood of educators creating the kinds of playful learning environments that privilege personal culture, interest and experience over demonstrable achievement. Educators will instinctively seek to 'manage' those environments in order to plan and regularly expose children to adult-directed activities that 'stand a better chance' (we might suppose) of revealing learning against prescribed outcomes. However, an overly directed, adult-led activity contains little inherent likelihood of connecting with the potentially diverse thematic interests of any individual child or group of children at any point in time. We might 'kid ourselves' that 'making it playful' will help to cultivate their interests, and indeed 'making it playful' might draw the children to the activity (as opposed to 'commanding them to attend'), but whether it will then subsequently engage the children in a meaningful learning process will depend on the extent to which the activity chimes with the children's cultural and intellectual interests at that particular point in time. At the ages of four and five, children are inherently driven to make sense of their world through exploration, language and thought. To overly direct their play is to make the learning experience meaningless for them. The Tickell Review (DoE 2011: 6) has recently made a recommendation to reduce the 117 learning outcomes to 20 'pieces of information to capture a child's level of development 'in a much less burdensome way'. It may be less 'burdensome' but huge numbers of subtleties and complexities in children's play are going to be missed if educators continue to focus only on the 'required measures'.

The EYFS Profile Handbook (QCA 2008: 15) takes a particular interest in the perceived underachievement of boys as compared with girls in relation to the national picture on EYFS profiling evident at this time. It clearly indicates that the environment may have a part to play in this:

> The EYFS profile provides a rounded picture of children's development and learning. National data shows that boys attain less well than girls across all areas of learning and that more girls are working securely within the early learning goals than boys. The difference is particularly marked in communication, language and literacy, and may in part reflect that the learning experiences on offer may not capture the interests or allow for the energy of some children. When building provision, practitioners should consider whether they are incorporating a wide enough range of activities to address these issues.
>
> Practitioners must create the right conditions for all children to demonstrate and develop their capabilities. Central to this is finding out what motivates children and what helps them continue to be interested, excited and motivated to learn. This can be as simple as asking them and doing something about it. The accuracy of EYFS profile assessments depends on the quality of observations of children engaged in self-initiated activities. For children to have the confidence to show initiative, their contributions and ways of learning must be valued and provided for. This requires provision that enables them to flourish regardless of their learning style, whether quiet or exuberant, preferring the outdoors or the classroom, methodical or favouring trial and error.

There are some interesting messages about flexibility and choice for children (or is it just boys?) in terms of how their learning environment is structured and resourced within this quote, but they seem difficult to tease out in any practical way. Also, set against the remainder of a handbook that aims to exemplify the measurement and moderation process in some considerable detail, one might forgive early years practitioners for not quite tuning into this important but rather cryptic quote. Certainly, during our many conversations in the setting and as we watched the filmed material, Andy reflected on the physicality of some boys, 'the rumbustiousness of their extended play'. He felt strongly that, if this were suppressed during their school experiences, it would detrimentally affect their self identity and their self esteem; the qualities that make them the children they are and the adults they become. Equally he felt that 'setting up activities designed to test their abilities' was a time-consuming and artificial act that held no guarantee of demonstrating any of the children's complex capabilities. What this meant was that the team devoted a considerable time to observing and recording the evidence of learning that was 'held within' the children's play activities; this key aspect of observation will be returned to later in the chapter.

In relation to the issues around the under-achievement of boys we would not want to endorse any generalised views here. As Connolly (2004: 33) points out, there is a real danger in oversimplifying these complex issues. For example, he points out that data suggests that the gaps between girls' and boys' achievements are closing. He advises against generalisations that 'hormones' or 'differing brain structures' can explain why 'girls are good at language' and why 'boys like to be active'. Part of the ongoing debate he points out has focussed on making schools more 'boy-friendly', which certainly seems to chime with the quote above and also with Andy's aspirations. In his book, Connolly explores these complexities at much greater depth than we can do justice here but we would certainly seek to avoid any notions of stereotyping the behaviours of boys and girls. As Epstein and colleagues (2001) discuss, what may seem like 'gendered preferences' often result from embedded cultural influences and unchallenged distributions of power. McNaughton (2000) also makes a compelling case for reconceptualising early childhood pedagogies in her research by showing how the traditional discourses of early childhood mitigate against gender equity.

It is worth briefly reflecting back on vignettes 1 and 2 in Chapter 1 (Archie and Luke designing their outdoor spaces) and vignette 6 in Chapter 3 (the five girls with their lizards). We cannot generalise from these examples and are not by any means claiming that girls use language more than boys, but there are interesting contrasts in that Archie and Luke build their play in these instances around actions and design with sporadic conversation, and the five girls build it around language and conversation with sporadic action. Their respective learning modes are quite distinctive on these particular occasions. However, the girls involved in the 'lizard conversation' are also involved with Debbie in vignette 6 (Chapter 3), where, in conjunction with Debbie, they combine conversations and design. Also, when Archie and Luke watched themselves on film, their conversations were rich and exploratory; it would be counter-productive in terms of seeking to understand the complexities of play if stereotypes were to be unthinkingly applied.

So what *should* adults be doing in playful learning environments?

What does all this mean for educators who have a requirement for checking children's learning in relation to pre-determined outcomes on one hand, and a commitment to working within a playful and liberating learning environment on the other hand? This is not a simple question, is it? This book and this chapter have no simple answers but we can talk about what evolved in the early years unit at Fishergate as the staff team themselves confronted these demands and dilemmas. Before we go on to look in some detail at the ways in which adults at Fishergate are thinking, acting and interacting, it may be helpful to have some sense of the daily routines and, in preliminary fashion at this point, indicate which periods of time were used for observation and staff discussions around playful learning:

8.45 a.m. Children and parents/carers are arriving and registration takes place. Elizabeth meets and greets and enters names in the register. Nursery children place their name in a basket with their parent's help, and reception children sign their names on a small whiteboard. Children enter and select indoor activities. All staff are welcoming and settling children and chatting with parents.

9.00 a.m. A whole class discussion time led by Andy. Children might be explaining what they were doing the previous day and/or planning the coming day. They might discuss what had happened at home. Andy might have selected something from the internet, linked to something children had been doing the previous day to discuss with the whole class (see Andy's reflection below).

9.15 a.m. Number work for reception children with Andy. Nursery children would be selecting indoor activities. As numbers grow over the school year the outdoor area might be opened up at this point to keep the noise levels lower for the reception children. Sometimes the reception children work with Andy in the main room but if the spare classroom is free they would move to this.

9.30 a.m. The reception children would now be choosing activities indoors or outside. Adults might be table-based at a free choice activity for children or observing/engaging with children in their play. Adults focus on the children in their key person groups but also tune into the activities of other children and discuss/point things out with and to team members. Key points are noted on sticky labels that go into the child's personal learning journey book, at which both parents and children can look, at any time of their choosing. Photos are often taken, printed off and also included in the books.

11.00 a.m. Snack time for children in their key person groups with conversation, and all children would help to tidy up at 11.15 a.m. It is perhaps worth inserting an observational note from Pat here from one of her visits:

As I watch the children in their key person groups having fruit and a drink, there's a strong sense of friendship. Their key person talks to each of them about what they have been doing today; others listen and also ask questions of one another. There's a lot of eye contact and smiling, hugging, watching, listening, helping. There's a lot of communication and language by adult and children.

(Pat's observational notes: 16 January)

11.30 a.m.	Reception children have their phonics time and nursery children have a story time.
11.45 a.m.	End of session for nursery children. Reception children might have a story or group time here and go for lunch at 12.00 p.m. and into the primary playground after lunch.
12.45 p.m.	Nursery children arrive.
1.00 p.m.	Reception children have their handwriting time with Andy, usually doing letter formation and sentence-level work.
1.15–2.30 p.m.	Reception children join the nursery children in the unit for free choice provision indoors and outdoors.
2.30 p.m.	Tidy-up time.
2.45–3.15 p.m.	Whole class story time and reflections on the day. This might include forward planning with the children relating to what they might do the next day: Have you thought about . . . ? Maybe you could . . . I wonder what would happen if . . . It was interesting when . . . Can you remember what happened when you . . . ?

Thinking, acting, interacting and discussion: learning from and providing for playful experiences

This reflection from Andy illustrates how observations of the children's play prompted him to begin to think differently about the complex notion of 'planning from children's interests'.

Andy reflects:

I saw that a group of three girls had taken pieces of coloured chalk from the large blackboards outside and had started to draw on the big army tyres as they lay flat on the ground. They noticed that the sides of the tyres had ridges and began to colour them in different colours. A smaller tyre was laid inside the bigger tyre and planks leaned across the large tyre. Some might be sitting inside the tyre and others working from the outside. There was some talk but not a lot, but everyone seemed to know what they were each doing. This was the first time I had noticed such play and watched with interest. Over about an hour, they covered the side of the tyre systematically and created, in effect, a work of art. Whilst the finished product is highly impressive, it seemed that, for the three girls, it was more about working together and feeling the chalk working down as it went over the ridges.

I took a lot of photographs and thought about their achievements in relation to the EYFS. I felt I'd seen something powerful where learning was going on but I wondered what my role was. Do I do nothing? Do I add something? I decided to search the internet and typed in 'tyre pictures'. Amongst the pictures were tyre sculptures of animals. I quickly found monster trucks with tyres on that were bigger than our army tyres and showed these to all the children (about 30 three- to five-year-olds) next day. I showed photos of the girls' play and their creation first of all, followed by what I had found on the net. I was trying to signal that I thought their play was important and that their ideas were also used by other people. A little while later, I did something similar with milk crates, looking on the net, and found some amazing structures including huge figures made of crates and a house made out of crates. I was amazed and genuinely interested in what I found and the children seemed to begin to understand how these pictures linked to their play as I talked to them about it.

From his observations, and genuine interest in the children's play, Andy had moved on to personal research and a new form of lesson-planning; creating an opportunity for a whole class experience to make links between their play experiences in the outdoor area and the wider world of art and culture. There were other occasions when the children's play prompted him to look for ways of extending their understanding through whole class activities using images and discussion.

On another occasion and over a number of weeks, the early years team observed the children as they explored slopes and gradients in lots of different ways. The children used narrow planks, running up and down them. They explored slopes by resting planks and wooden boards on different levels. They explored the slopes in a range of physical ways, riding bikes, running and sliding down the slopes, walking up slopes. The team discussed and analysed what the children's interests were and what learning was taking place. They did this on a large whiteboard in the classroom where team members also record children's interests against their names (Figures 4.1 and 4.2). The parents look at this and occasionally add to it also with related activities that children have undertaken at home. It becomes a composite record which remains for a few days before other children are focussed upon.

Drawing from their analysis of these activities, the team thought about ways to extend and support the ongoing learning. They wanted to show the children that the concepts they were exploring were used in the wider world and that there were some scientific ideas at work here in their play.

As part of their planning–reflection process team members listed on the whiteboard what the children were doing: using gradients, slopes, different speeds and the feelings of going faster and slower as they went slowly up slopes on a bike and 'whooshed' down the other side. They then discussed how the sensations would feel for the children. They identified in their discussions roller coasters and fairground rides as possible sources of these experiences – probably drawing here on their own memories. Andy researched this on the net and found footage on the Blackpool pleasure beach website of the roller coaster. It was presented as though the viewer was sitting on and experiencing the roller coaster and he showed this to the whole class. The children thought it was funny, exciting and interesting. They recognised links between what they were seeing

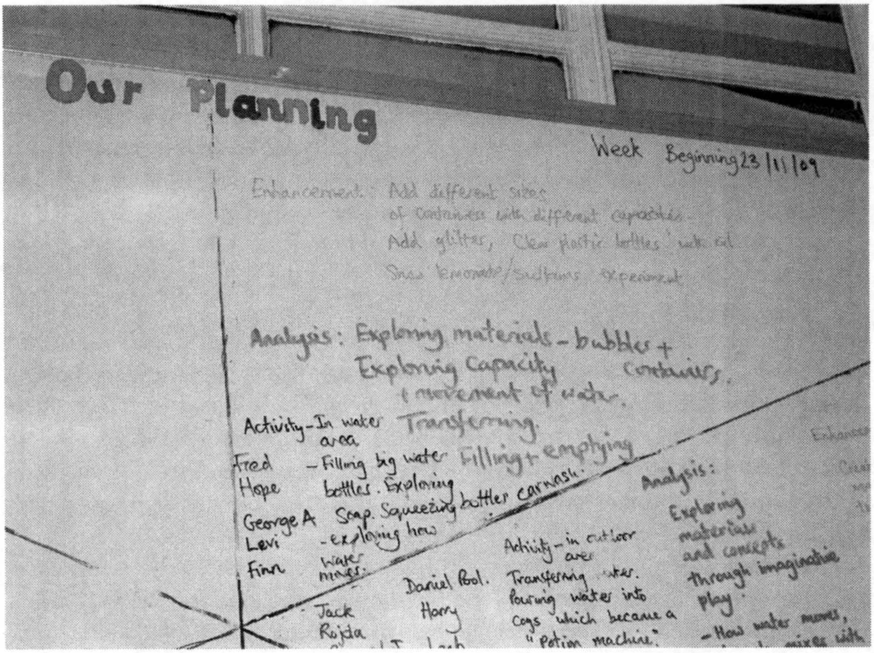

Figure 4.1 Recording plans on the whiteboard.

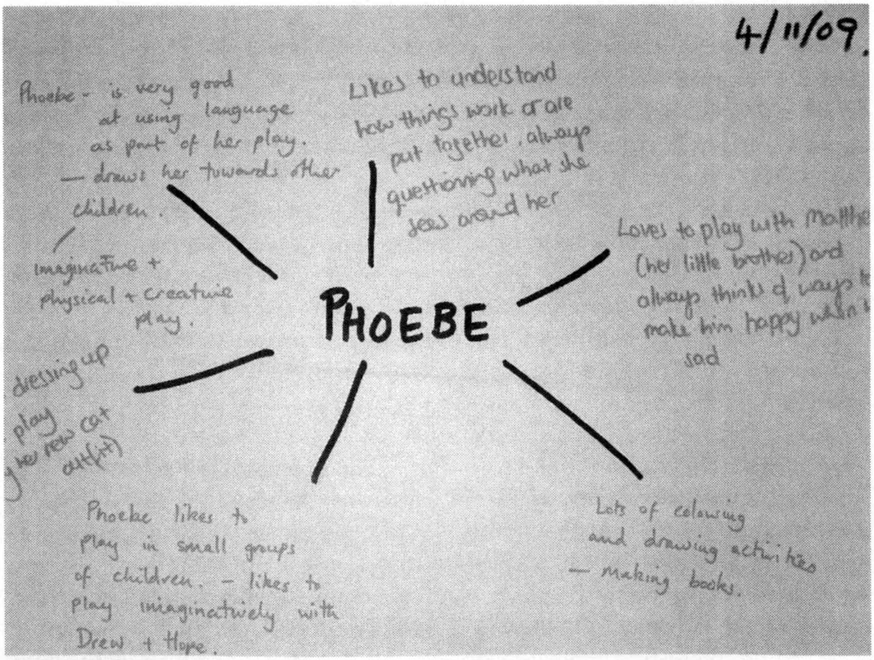

Figure 4.2 Recording interests on the whiteboard.

and what they had been doing in the outdoor area and Andy also elaborated on these links for them. It led to lots of discussion about how it made you feel, about safety, about why people do not fall out, about speed, about the effects of the slopes on the ride. In the course of the discussion, Andy then fetched a small bucket of water and demonstrated centrifugal force to them by swinging it around his head. The five-year-olds were subsequently seen trying this experiment themselves; this has also been captured on film and was something that some children were interested in over several weeks. The team noticed the extent to which it captured the older children's interests and it reinforced for them practical ways in which children's interests could form the basis of a taught experience.

This next reflection concerns a conversation between Pat and Rachel as, whilst watching outdoor play together, they reflected on this business of the adult's role in relation to children's free-choice, playful activities. It is offered as Pat's reflection.

Rachel and I were watching a reception boy pulling another boy across the outdoor area. He was hauling on a long rope that he had tied to a large plastic shape with holes, in which his friend was sitting, laughing and encouraging him to go faster. He pulled the rope around the corner of a low wall and tried to haul the boy-shape after him. The rope was stuck in a cement gap between the bricks. He pulled harder; nothing happened. He investigated and then released the rope from the crack but still he could not pull the plastic shape because of the angle of the rope to the heavy shape. He went to get more children to help him pull but still they couldn't move the shape with the boy inside around the corner. The boy inside was patient and encouraging and they tried different placements on the rope. What they needed to do was to shorten the rope but they didn't arrive at this conclusion; they thought that 'force' as represented by more children would bring a solution.

As we watched, Rachel and I discussed the problem-solving techniques that were being devised and we both recognised what the solution should be. We talked about whether we should demonstrate the solution or not or perhaps try and help them think it through, although we did feel that an awful lot of thinking and discussion was ongoing without us and getting them to understand why a shorter rope would work might not be the conceptual space they were inhabiting. It might solve the immediate problem but perhaps be ultimately meaningless within their wider understandings – but also, perhaps not – we just didn't know.

Eventually, the boy pulling the rope gave up and walked away; the other children left also and the boy inside the shape got out and followed his friend indoors.

Once more we reflected on whether we should have intervened to scaffold the play and to help them 'succeed'. Rachel was not concerned that they hadn't found a solution because she felt that if they were really interested in solving the problem – and they seemed so – they would come back to it at some point, although quite possibly at a point when no adult was watching them, so we may never know whether they solved the problem. Does that matter? we wondered. It made us realise that it was about trusting the environment to create the opportunities for problem-setting and solving but also about regular observations to check that this was happening.

Working alongside the children: designing, building and playing in the boat

This next activity was initiated by Debbie following on from her observations the previous day when these five girls had worked together in the outdoor area making a train from logs and other natural materials. She had asked the group of girls if they would like to design and make something indoors and said that she would help. They decided on a boat. They began by drawing around plastic bricks on a large sheet of paper on the floor to get the outline of the boat and to think about its size. This took them quite a long time, half an hour, and they understood the need for precision in keeping the drawings to the edge of the large piece of paper (from a roll) that they were working on, to allow space 'inside' the boat for the passengers. They had ongoing discussions about how many people they would want in the boat. When they needed to turn the corner on the design, in discussion with Debbie, one of the children suggested they could use the curved bricks, which were ideal. They found larger bricks to draw around to represent where the seats would be located inside the boat.

Once they had agreed the size and the outline design, the children decided, with discussion initiated by Debbie, that they would need 'paddles' (meaning oars). She suggested they find materials to make the paddles and left them exploring the indoor and outside materials; she came back occasionally to check their progress. This involved pairs and small groups in conversations around the usefulness or uselessness of the range of materials available. The children eventually decided, as a group, and without an adult prompt, to use plastic rakes, anchored with tape inside cardboard tubes, for the paddles and agreed they would need four. There was quite a long discussion around how long the paddles needed to be and what size of cardboard tubes should be used; they compared several sizes, with related discussions. The boat had been designed but not built by lunchtime (Figure 4.3) and the girls decided they would like to finish it in the afternoon.

Debbie did not initially find it easy to engage with the children in this play and said she had really had to think about how her role should be shaped, how much direction she should give and how she might move the play forward and sustain the children's interests through achievement without overly directing them. She reflected later as we were watching the video: 'I felt at times that I was leading too much. I didn't want to put ideas in their heads. I felt it would be good if we had some pictures of boats', which she had subsequently provided for the children to study.

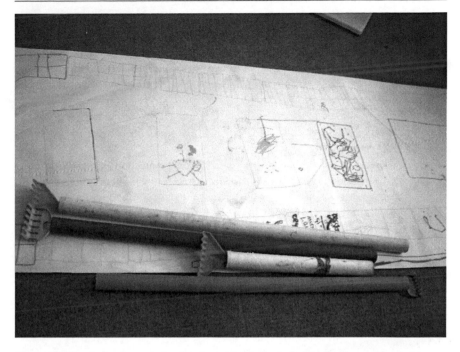

Figure 4.3 The design is made by drawing around plastic bricks for the outline and larger shapes for seating.

At snack time, during the morning as the design stage was ongoing, we had taken the children to look at the filming of their boat designing. Their commentaries reflected the different stages of their activity and, to some extent, the issues they were thinking about as they worked. Unless otherwise stated, these comments come from different children as they watched the film and demonstrate the level and quality of the children's ongoing thinking as the boat took shape:

> This was when you got stuck (*drawing around a plastic block on the paper*).
>
> Yes, it was too small to get it on the paper. (*They were right to the edge of the large piece of paper and using curved bricks to create 'corners'.*)
>
> There was no room.
>
> If we had drawn all of them (*the outlines of all the bricks needed for the boat*) it would have been too slow (*reiterating here comments that Debbie had made to them as they designed the boat*).
>
> We waited till we saw something we wanted and then we thought we could get some more (*as they look for paddles*).
>
> We are going to build it this afternoon because this is the design. (*They are very clear about the shorter- and longer-term aspects of the activity; a clear sense of goals is apparent.*) Will you video us building it?
>
> *Pat:* Do you want me to?

Yes.

Pat: Then I will.

We can't have Rebecca in the boat; she's not here this afternoon. (*This is about planning the use of the boat, which has been an integral part of the design. They are building the boat for themselves to use in ongoing play; it is not perceived as a task to 'please the teacher'; it's their task and will be used for their purposes.*)

Look (*points at herself on the film*), I'm looking for Rebecca to go in the boat (*see Rebecca's case study in Chapter 6; this search for Rebecca is captured on film as well*).

I've been on a red boat on the river (*drawing from personal memories*).

Yeah; I've been on a boat on the river too (*related memories stimulated*).

Yeah, yeah and I have (*more personal recollections of real experiences*).

The seats were too big so I got one big one and two little ones (*talking about the seats she is trying to fit into the boat design they have been making; she is drawing around blocks that will become seats but anticipating 'fit'*).

Maybe we could get the blue one (*a smaller seat elsewhere in the unit; this shows how well this girl has mentally catalogued the available resources in the unit*).

Yeah and look, we're writing the names of the people coming in our boat (*as they make their list – purposeful writing as an incidental but important part of their activity*).

In relation to purposeful writing, in her reflections during interview, Vicky made the following comment when asked by Pat, 'Do you think this environment stretches the older children?':

That's something I was unsure about, with the general reading and writing and those sorts of things. But then I see some of the things they do and their writing is just phenomenal. The more able children just push themselves. I have the feeling that the unit gives them enough and they leave really inspired and motivated . . . I think they'll cope well with the transition to Year 1 because they are ready to fly with it . . . the language and stories that some come out with, what they have imagined and done and built is definitely stretching them. I've been impressed.

The building of the boat occurred in the afternoon. Debbie suggested that they moved their design into the large construction area so that they could look at it, as they built their boat alongside it. This they did, checking against their design every so often and discussing amongst themselves what they would do next. At one point, Debbie assisted by passing the bricks to them; this helped to speed up the building part of the task. When completed, the children began a series of play activities, as a group, in the boat with as many as nine children involved at times. Throughout the day, the same group of five children had remained together and they invited other children into the completed boat;

Rebecca is much younger than the builders, who are reception-aged children, but was an important part of the play. The themes clearly had intrinsic interest for them; their original idea had been to build a boat, and several of them, it emerged as we watched the film, have been on boats – this is York and the River Ouse runs through the centre of the city and, in recent years, has often flooded. It is quite possibly a key feature of their lives, a source of possible danger as well as one of fun and excitement with other family members. Their group commitment to the play, which lasted a day and proceeded through the designing, building and using stages, strongly suggests a convergent play theme; a place and space where they engaged in long conversations with an adult and with peers, where they set and solved problems together and where they achieved a goal that gave voice to a highly cooperative play activity involving expert and younger players.

Debbie may have been uncertain about her role because this was a new way of working for her, but she was in no doubt at the end of the day that it had been highly beneficial for the children. The challenge for Debbie had been to draw a distinction, through her actions, interactions and discussions with the children, between imposing her own ideas on the children and instead finding ways of liberating the children's ideas; ideas clearly chiming with real experiences outside school for several of the children. The children are learning to lead complex and extended play narratives as they exercise the 'right to roam' around their play environment in the selection of the right materials to extend their design ideas and to further develop their own understanding of the world around them. As the activity had progressed, Debbie had left the children for longer periods, although she did stay with them during the design stage, checking that they understood the purposes of the design. Because of other responsibilities around the unit, it was only when we watched the film together with the children that she was able to understand the full extent of the children's independent commitment to the activity as they progressed the boat in her absence and to see that it had been a very purposeful and enjoyable activity for them.

What Debbie is learning for herself here is that learning to follow the children's collective agenda and personal interests requires the adult to think in new ways, as well as acting in new ways. In her final interview, Debbie reflected on her own progress and personal development in terms of new ways of looking at and thinking about children's play and said:

> I think I have developed into a nicer person, a much more positive person I think. I think that's through chatting with others and watching. Seeing the best in children. Not thinking – that child's making a mess that I've got to clear up at the end of the morning but seeing that the child is learning from the activity. Once, for example, with magic potions, I used to think: 'Oh my word I've got to tidy that up' but now I think 'Wow, look at what they're using, what else have we got that they might want, what about the glitter?'

It is also very interesting that this was a group of girls involved for such a long period in a 'design and build' activity; they are also good friends, as these were some of the girls in the 'lizard conversation' of vignette 6 in Chapter 3. We have seen girls involved with boys in design activities and it would also be true to say that much of what we captured on film relating to design did involve pairs or groups of boys, usually outdoors. It is interesting to speculate that it may have been the *continued presence and interest* of Debbie with this group of girls that constituted the encouragement they needed to pursue their 'design and build' goals for so long. Unlike, for example, the Archie and Luke vignettes of Chapter 2, which resulted in complex designs but involved comparatively less language between the boys, this day-long boat-building activity involved constant conversations between the girls themselves and of the girls with Debbie when she was present.

In the afternoon, the girls watched themselves again in the film of their play. Here they had progressed from 'design and build' to their boat-related play scenarios. Their comments show their parallel interests in describing and explaining the play and its purposes as well as exploring their feelings and memories from other events during the play:

Look Ali; you're there; this is after snack time.
　　There's Rosie and there's you.
　　I wanted five seats.
　　We took the seats out when we wanted to lie down.
　　I wasn't very happy because I wasn't allowed to paddle the boat.
　　We didn't want you to paddle.
　　Lucy told me to come.
　　No, we found you and asked you to come.
　　Lucy's sitting in the bottom bit.
　　I explain, design, then build (*demonstrating a clear understanding of the development of the day-long activity*).
　　She said put my feet there and it would be comfortable.
　　A pet was in the box (*a rapid shift from the 'real' to the imagined; these aspects are closely inter-connected as the thinking and discussion flows*).
　　We're rowing the boat and I'm sinking because I needed to mend the paddle.
　　We're going for a walk.
　　No, a drown (*quick-thinking humour from Lucy, followed by laughter; Lucy enjoys good natured teasing and making others laugh, which was evident also in vignette 5 in Chapter 3*).
　　I'm sellotaping 'cos I need to wrap it round (*as the paddle is repaired*).
　　Lucy was being sick (*playful*).
　　Timothy and Zack were sick at home and I was sick on the doorstep (*real memories*).
　　I was sick in my bed (*another real memory to be reflected upon*).

We're putting sellotape on the rake to hold it on.

I'm telling Tina to get off Pearl.

Tina, you keep falling on me.

Yeah.

That was really funny (*shared humorous experience that is part of their friendship*).

I was pretend sellotaping my mouth (*Lucy again, the humorous part of her character still to the fore*).

It took us ages and ages to do the paddle (*their completion of the paddles showed real persistence; the design was very challenging, they understand the quality of their own commitment and there is a real sense of achievement depicted here*).

That's us going for a walk (*a strong sense of community and sharing; the children do also go for walks as a class*).

This is incredibly vibrant language these five-year-olds are engaging with and it reveals the richness of their inner lives and the relevance of recent memories, along with a clear sense of goal achievement and friendship, as expressed within this play activity. It is also possible that what these children are showing, as perhaps have other children who have previously reflected on their play in this research, is a capacity for *self-regulation* and *meta-cognition* (the capacity to know that one is thinking in order to solve problems). These abilities were originally thought to be only evident in much older children but work by Robson (2010), and Whitebread and colleagues (2007) have shown evident capacities in much younger children 'in naturally occurring social contexts which have meaning and purpose for children' (Robson 2010: 228). In this boat-building scenario, the children are demonstrating that they know what they know about the design and build activity, they know that they are using this knowledge and they are able to understand the emotional aspects of their play because they can identify them and draw them to attention. They are able to recognise and understand their own problem-solving behaviours which occur naturally in their playful activities in a meaningful context – a context stimulated by an adult but one that also parallels their own life experiences and interests.

Student teachers in the open-ended play environment

Andy is aware that the open-ended nature of the play environment presents especial challenges for student teachers, not least in relation to their planning. The traditional planning model of today's student teachers is to devise mid-term plans before the placement begins and then daily planning activities in advance of each day in order to show breadth and balance in the planning and to demonstrate a clear understanding of the concept of 'intended learning outcomes'. What has evolved at Fishergate is a move away from the planning of intended learning outcomes to the provision of an environment that allows children, with appropriate adult support, to determine their own learning outcomes and to pursue them at length and in depth. As we illustrated with Archie and Luke's vignettes and as we will return to in Chapter 6, this in-depth immersion showed progression in playful learning, not over days, but over weeks and months. Learning is slow, progressive and purposeful and this sits in direct contradiction to notions of establishing activities to measure summative gains in order to fulfil external requirements for meeting standards.

As we have seen from the boat episode above, the early years team do plan to engage with the children in activities, but these are of the children's own devising and draw from their immediate experiences and memories. Debbie, above did not have a plan 'to design and build a boat with the children'; it originated from their interests although she did initiate the conversation by linking into previous, observed activities and the idea for it was stimulated through team discussions the previous day. However, seeing its relevance to the children, she may well, in the future, seed it as a possibility, perhaps using books, to see if it 'takes root' in a desire, by the children, to design and play with the idea. However, as we have also seen, the capacity to think and act in this way as a teacher has to be learned and the students will have similar developmental needs to take into account as part of their own learning process in the setting.

The early years team have also come to understand that, at particular times of the year, particular interests are pursued by the children. These are often, for example, related to the weather, with windy days prompting interests in designing kites, warm days in finding mini-beasts and building 'homes' for them, and icy days in exploring the changes that warm and cold can make to the environment. The staff can plan to exploit these conditions in developing children's activities and experiences but this is largely because they have been there long enough to see how the weather cycles are an integral and, for the children, interesting part of what they might do as the year progresses. Although it may not be possible to predict what children can be interested in, they have learned through observation and discussion as a staff team that key themes are revisited. They also do planned activities such as vegetable and shrub planting, filling the bird feeders, building a pirate ship, providing materials for mixing magic potions, and demonstrating how the pulley system installed on the wall and the guttering can be used for transporting water. Many of these now planned-for activities have developed from noting the frequency of different children's interests in these aspects of the environment. The team have the advantage of time to watch and reflect together to build their own understandings and so inform their planned activities in terms of assisting children in their skill-building in using the resources around them and in realising that they have implicit permission to move resources from one place to another.

Student teachers, however, have a fixed period of time to demonstrate their competences, and Andy and the team have come to recognise that some student teachers seem to 'get' what they are working for in the setting whereas others, initially at least, struggle to understand what their role should be. Andy feels it is a similar experience for visitors to the unit and occasionally for supply teachers:

some visitors understand its potential immediately and others seem to see only chaos, especially during the extended open-ended play periods available to the children. Elizabeth made an astute reflection during interview, about visitors, showing how she acknowledges the concerns they have as concerns that the team members in the unit also had, before their own understanding of children's learning began to shift:

> We get so many visitors from other schools. Some will say: 'Oh we can't do that in our classrooms.' And we'll say: 'Well, we didn't think we could, but we could.'

Planning for the more formal group times relating to literacy and numeracy seems less challenging to adults and so, in some ways, safer territory – other than the ongoing but no less substantial challenge of ensuring the activities are interesting for the children and can address the wide range of abilities that will inevitably be present.

Kat was one student teacher who did 'get it', but this was over time and with structured support that could take her from a clearly defined role in engaging with the children in an open-ended play environment to her understanding how to operate in support of children's play themes rather than in initiation of them, and, in addition, thinking about the ways in which one might 'plan' for the different kinds of activities. This planning needs to focus on exploiting the possibilities in relation to one's role in working with the children, rather than planning for specific learning outcomes as being directly related to specifically planned activities. We will try and illustrate this a little more clearly by taking two instances in Kat's work with the children, the first at the beginning of her placement and the second towards the end of her placement.

Taking an open-ended role in a specific play area

It was suggested to Kat by Andy that she become engaged with the children at the workbench and that she plan for the development and maintaining of this area, which would include observing how the children used it, in order to inform her planning. This was a new area of provision for the children and it was clear that quite a few children would need to develop their skills in using hammers and saws, hammering in nails and so on. In this next vignette, we offer an account of the filmed activity on the left and Kat's own account of events on the right, as she watched the film later. In the centre we also offer a brief comment from Zack, the four-year-old boy involved. When Pat asked him, Zack said he did not want to watch the film on the large screen but said he would watch it on the small screen on the camera, which he did. We have also included a reference to Zack's dinosaur play because it is worth noting his long-standing interest as expressed through his play at Fishergate, and also to understand the flow of play as children decide to cease one activity and begin another. What may look on the face of it to be an arbitrary decision on Zack's part to stop one activity and begin another, may in fact be a deliberate decision as a memory of the previous day's activity in the woodwork area returns to him.

Vignette 7

The filmed account	Zack's comments	Kat's reflections (after the initial comment on 'dinosaurs')
Zack is playing with Mathilda and Emma running outside: 'Stand back, there's a dinosaur, it's wild; stand back.' All three run around the large outdoor space in a line. They run into an enclosed den area continuing the theme of 'hiding from the dinosaur'. They run back across the yard shouting and return to their starting point, continuing a dialogue about dinosaurs. They jump into puddles and then all three go indoors; Zack leads the way.	We have to battle it and run away. Then that dinosaur was coming to get me.	There is evidence of Zack's interest in dinosaurs going back to at least eight months previously with photos of models he has made on the wall.
All three children go over to the woodwork bench and Zack gets a drill. Kat is there and begins to talk to him about what he is making. He begins to drill and the two girls are watching. One begins to select pieces of wood. Zack works with Kat for over 20 minutes and makes a complex boat which he then	I went in 'cos I wanted to play with the, the, the hammer. I wanted to make a boat. I seen them somewhere and been reading 'bout them. *Pat:* Why are you making the hole? *Zack:* To put the sail on. When I got to	Kat said that Zack said, at first, that he wanted to make a river, then a car, but there were no wheels so 'I suggested a boat' and he said 'yes', and thought of all the ideas after that. He wanted sails and a cannon; he wanted a mast. He'd not really been in that area before but yesterday we decided to have an adult in

takes over to the water tray to 'test'. It falls on its side and he discusses this with Kat and with Andy as he passes and looks at the boat. Zack returns to try some new ideas for keeping it upright. One girl leaves but another girl remains for a long period watching Zack and working beside him, using the drill and selecting pieces of wood. As he tests out his boat again in the water tray, a small group of boys gather round watching; they join in their discussions about why it might be falling over. He returns to the work bench with Kat to continue working on it.

the drill then it was broken and I had to get another one. I was, was, was thinking that I needed to make some more holes, holes.

the area and nine children went in and it worked better. They don't really know how to use the things. So he came in yesterday and today he came back in again and was saying 'I like building things' and 'I'm really good at this, aren't I?' The boat was falling over and we were talking about that and Rob, who had come to watch, said we needed some holes in the stern, so we went back to do some more work on it. Mr Burt also suggested a rudder so we did that. When he'd done it Zack said he thought we should leave it in the water area for other people. When he came in this morning he was asking me to help him with the hammering again.

EYFS learning outcomes

PSRN: Use developing mathematical ideas and methods to solve practical problems.

PSRN: Use language such as 'greater', 'smaller', 'heavier' or 'lighter' to compare quantities.

KUW: Ask questions about why things happen and how things work.

Kat demonstrates her understanding of her changing perceptions of her role and of its impact on the quality of the children's play as she commented to me after we had watched the film: 'It's really great to get in there with them and just be accepted, much better than leading an actual activity.' Before we move on to look at how Kat is working later in the placement, it is also worth mentioning Zack's preoccupation with 'rivers' and to wonder yet again if this is the cultural impact upon him of living in the city. In Chapter 5 we return to Zack again as he makes a 'rainbow river' in the outdoor area with friends; even so, this seemingly new interest sits alongside a continuing interest in dinosaurs that has lasted almost a year so far for Zack.

In the next extract we follow and reflect on Kat's changing style as a teacher. Here she is in the outdoor space, with no specifically planned remit other than to observe the children and make judgements about when/how she might begin to engage with them as a co-player.

Vignette 8

Archie, Luke and the telescope

Reflections on Kat's role as educator and on Archie and Luke's play

Archie and Luke have made a design with cable reels and crates in the centre of the outdoor area. A long, wide plastic tube has been stood on end on one of the reels. Luke goes indoors and returns with food and a saucepan and says: 'On a tea break we can eat one of these.' Luke is cooking; Archie is walking around and there is inaudible conversation and pretend eating. The film captures the end of a conversation between Archie and Kat. Archie points to the tube and says: 'We didn't tie that up.' Kat asks: 'Is it not a telescope any more?' Archie looks at the plastic tube, rubs his forehead and says: 'Well it could be.' He continues discussing it but his voice is inaudible. Later Archie is arranging the resources in the design; then he sits and looks at the 'telescope' for a few minutes.

Archie has located the telescope (the tube) but Luke seems not to understand the concept and is engaged in a domestic play theme. Archie seems deep in thought, perhaps trying to develop the telescope play theme. Kat is aware of the telescope theme and asks a genuine question as the telescope play seems to have been replaced by domestic play, but, as Archie's ongoing comments and subsequent actions show, he remains interested in the theme.

Filming recommences and Archie is explaining to Kat his visit to a telescope and how he 'went under it and I looked up through it'. Kat replies 'Ah, so you want to look up through it' and she moves to the 'telescope' and asks 'What will we see when we look through it?' Archie replies 'You might see some satellites' and continues his reflection but also seems to be thinking hard. Kat is lifting down the telescope from its previous position and says: 'I'll need some help with this, I think.'

Luke asks Archie shall they paint the 'table'. Archie looks at the telescope and nods to Luke; Luke skips off to get the paints and Archie looks across at Kat, who is standing by the tube looking at it. She calls to Luke that there are paints outside if he wants them. Archie goes across to get a pot of paint and he and Luke return to paint the table. The telescope is laid on the floor and Kat leaves the boys to their painting. She picks up a clipboard on which she makes occasional notes of what the children are engaged with. Luke and Archie talk as they paint but Archie also looks across at the tube/telescope on the floor and then asks 'Shall I paint this one?', referring to another reel. Luke says 'Yes'; they continue with sporadic conversation and keep going till the reels are painted to their satisfaction.

Filming moves inside but, on return, Kat and Archie are each moving two towers of three crates across the outdoor area. Kat asks Archie where he wants them putting. He shows her. He places them parallel and quite close together; he asks Kat to lift the tube into the gap between the crates. This is quite high and he watches as Kat tries to

Archie uses explanations to try and tune Kat in to what he wants and she recognises and responds positively, realising that they need to relocate and raise the telescope if they are to look up through it.

Archie seems torn between the telescope and playing with Luke. Kat is sensitive to this and lays the tube on the floor as the play changes direction. She makes no attempt to coax Archie into the telescope play but follows his lead. She records their play interests on the clipboard and later on Archie picks it up too and 'writes' on it.

Kat has responded again to Archie's desire to return to the telescope. She understands from the earlier conversation about 'looking up' that they need to lift the telescope and suspend it. Archie has suggested they use crates. As one watches the film manoeuvre the 'telescope' into its place. Archie seems to be checking the width of the space as she lowers it in. Andy is passing and sees that they may need help; the tube is heavy. They wedge it securely in and now the boys can go underneath it and look upwards. Archie does this first and then Luke copies.

and thinks about the 'thinking postures' that Archie has exhibited, it seems apparent that he has been mentally planning this design and trying to solve his design 'problems'.

Kat asks 'Can we see satellites?' Kat is still trying to ensure the tube is firm and suggests 'Maybe we should use some (inaudible) as well. There are some shorter tubes we could use.' Archie and Luke do not seem interested in her idea and go back under the telescope to look upwards. Kat is still holding tight to the sides to support the tube. A younger child has been watching and goes under himself to look upwards. Conversation continues with Kat; other children also come to look at the design.

Kat remembers what Archie has said they will see, thus valuing his earlier conversation. Luke seems to be getting the hang of the purpose of the design and other children also take an interest in getting beneath the tube and looking upwards.

After a while, Kat says she thinks she needs to let go and they must take it down as it will fall down when she lets go, but suggests they might try and think of other ways of building a safe telescope. Archie says 'We could use tyres.' He and Luke run off to get 'tyres, tyres, tyres' and begin wheeling them over. They wheel them around, getting out the water that has collected in them. They wait for Kat, who is helping children apply suntan lotion. Kat suggests removing one layer of crates 'to make it lower and safer' and then helps the boys lift the tyres on to the crates. Archie says: 'Do mine'. They have selected two different sizes of tyres. Archie inspects it and asks: 'Shall I get some more?'

Kat is genuinely tired of holding it but her open-ended suggestion prompts Archie to think of a way of making the construction safe and by now Luke understands enough about Archie's goals to help him.

Kat replies: 'Do you think you want some?' Luke brings another small tyre, which they put on the pile. Archie goes beneath the crates and arranges two crates to make 'doors' underneath the tyres.

Archie is uncertain but Kat encourages him to make the decision.

Archie then begins to make a ramp down the structure with guttering, and Kat continues to assist them as they and other children begin to fetch and pour water. They extend the ramp till it reaches the floor and Andy, who is passing, fetches a cement mixing tray to catch the water (Figure 4.4). The children bring a crate for Kat to stand on so she can reach the start of the 'water run', which, being longer, is now higher. This play continues for another half hour and eventually involves between seven and nine children pouring and watching the water. Children stand on crates beside Kat so they can pour water; others sit on crates beside the construction and watch.

Kat praises Archie as he puts two crates beneath the now very long 'guttering' ramp

Kat is flexible enough to allow and support the development of a new play theme.

Praise for good ideas is a common way in which other

Figure 4.4 The telescope is now a water carrier.

(two pieces have been overlapped) to stop it sagging: 'What a good idea, Archie, what a good idea.' She praises Luke for 'finding a big bottle instead of that little cup'; 'what a good idea'.

Kat asks Archie how full the collecting tray is. He stammers as he tries to find the words he wants: 'It's not too . . . it's not to the . . . it's not, it's not to the rim.' When he finds this final word a big smile spreads on his face and he looks with satisfaction at the tray of water. The play continues but Archie is watching now and others are using the design and talking to Kat.

team members engage with the children and Kat has taken this into her own repertoire of play engagement with the children.

Kat's question to Archie is meaningful and elicits an answer that shows good vocabulary and sheer pleasure for Archie in remembering this unusual word: 'rim'. A small perhaps but clearly meaningful moment for him.

EYFS learning outcomes

CLL: Be confident to try new activities, imitate ideas and speak in a familiar group.

PSE: Work as part of a group or class, taking turns and sharing fairly, understanding that there needs to be agreed values and codes of behaviour for groups of people, including adults and children, to work together harmoniously.

CD: Express and communicate their ideas thoughts and feelings by using a widening range of materials, suitable tools, imaginative and role play, movement, designing and making, (and a variety of songs and musical instruments).

It is interesting to consider whether any of the above activity would have occurred had an adult not been present. As with the boat 'design and build' activity, the adult's presence seems a key part here of activity development and the children's long-term engagement. In the above play, the materials were too heavy for Archie to lift alone and throughout, Kat is sensitive to, but not 'pushing', the telescope theme. Archie had visited a telescope recently, hence his capacity for conceptualising it and Luke's apparent mystification at what was going on until the point when he could get under the telescope and look through it at the sky. It seemed that, for Luke, realisation dawned at this point and he was able to engage with Archie in the design activity. Kat was sensitive and flexible enough to realise that the boys wanted to exploit the open-ended nature of the space and place to create something specific.

By this stage, Kat was developing her own conceptual understanding of the space as she commented: 'Because they get to choose whatever they want to do, then you know it's something they're interested in.' She was also able to articulate the demands on her as an educator as she said: 'There's been times when I've watched children doing something in the morning and, over dinner time, have added something to the area to try and extend what they were doing in the morning.'

This is a long way from sitting them down at an adult-designed activity to test the children's summative knowledge. What Kat is showing she understands here is the extent to which the environment itself, along with the resources, the time to play and the adult as observer and co-player can achieve in terms of a myriad of parallel learning outcomes. She has progressed over the course of her placement towards understanding the relationships between the adult's role and the children's interests in this learning environment. Let us look again at Table 0.1, which depicts the relationship between playful pedagogy on the left and playful learning on the right, to see how far Kat has come.

Through the reconceptualising of the planning process and by focussing assessment, through observation and conversation, on the children's interests, Kat, like the other members of the early years team, is now able to make informed decisions about when to engage, when to watch, when to listen, when to praise

Table 0.1 Playful pedagogies and playful learning: the juxtaposition model

'Open-ended play': understanding playful pedagogies	'The whatever you want it to be place': revealing playful learning

A way for the adult to conceive of her/ his own role in creating and sustaining an educational environment that is flexible enough to allow children's interests and experiences to emerge and develop; it also encompasses the adults' responsibilities in identifying, recording and planning for those interests in systematic but flexible ways and a responsibility to look for ways of extending those interests and relating them to the wider world in which the child is living and learning.
 	
    The early years setting becomes a space and place where adults nurture potential and push the boundaries of their personal understandings of playful learning and playful pedagogies.
	The environment and its possibilities as perceived and engaged with from the child's perspective. The child enters a space where anything is possible – whether a large or small space – and where they can engage alone or with others in exploring and exploiting that environment to match the images, plans and memories that emerge from their own minds, experiences and skills.
	
	    The early years setting becomes a space and place where children explore their identity, potential and interests and push back the boundaries of personal possibility through playful engagement.

and when to prompt. The impact of children's enthusiastic engagement on an individual's changing pedagogies is not a new phenomenon. Stephen (2010: 25) describes it in relation to Scottish teachers, who commented that it allowed them to spend more time with individual children and also that: 'Practitioners saw changes they had implemented as resulting in children being more engaged in and enthusiastic about learning and increasing in confidence and independence in the classroom.'

This is a comment that certainly chimes with life at Fishergate as described here by Jane:

> Pat: So what is it about learning through play here that gives them that independence? Is it resources, how the adults work, the amount of time they've got?
>
> Jane: I think it's a mixture of everything because we let them take the lead, we look at what they're interested in and we know how we can expand that or put the ideas there for them to work on. They're using their imagination more than if they just had climbing frames and bikes and they're making their own mistakes. They have to work things out for themselves, solve their own problems, 'if I do it this way, it might work', 'it might work if it goes down here'.

The next chapter now takes a look at risk and conflict within the pedagogies of play.

The pedagogies of risk and the value of conflict

Chapter 5 is presented in two sections; the inter-connections are explained in this opening section of the chapter. The first section examines risky play, including risk-taking both for children and for educators; it examines the permitting and encouragement of risk-taking and the calculating of risk by children and adults. The second section explores examples of conflict between peers and the children's responses to conflict, and also considers aspects of conflict resolution. The two sections of the chapter are connected in a number of ways. First, both risk and conflict are aspects of playful engagement about which adults – both educators and parents/carers – regularly express concerns. Health and safety are features of both aspects of play, with educators concerned about resulting injuries and, in addition, conflict raises a perceived potential for 'violence', which no one would advocate as relevant to an early years setting. Second, engaging in either risk or conflict and conflict resolution embodies a substantial element of independent action by a child or children. When children take risks or when they engage in conflicts, they are often quite unconcerned with adult perspectives or exhortations until these are imposed upon them by an intervening adult. Events associated with each scenario are exclusively child-focussed and 'of the moment' as the child makes a decision to act in a particular way – to take a risk or to engage in or respond to a situation of conflict. This can lead adults – especially anxious adults – to equate the actions with 'loss of control' by the child or perceived recklessness by the child.

Risky play

The following discussions aim to illustrate that, in either situations of risk-taking or conflict resolution at Fishergate, children are never reckless or out of control, during risk-taking or conflict. We would propose from study of the filmed material that has captured these aspects of play that, in relation both to risk-taking and conflict, there are degrees of calculation, thoughtfulness and self-regulation, by the children, in operation. Further, these opportunities for calculated risk, in relation to both risky play and conflict resolution, are essential features of the road to maturity for children – when they occur in settings where adults are seeking to create optimum opportunities for independent action and interaction; settings where adult leadership of play is minimised and where children's capacities to make choices that correspond with their interests and experiences are maximised.

In this next quote from her interview, Rachel captures the sense of uncertainty for the adult in working in a substantially child-initiated environment as follows:

> Yes, there is uncertainty and you've got to be flexible. In this way of working the adult isn't in control and that does make for some uncertainty. It can feel risky. As a teacher, you are normally there to teach the child, that's your role, you're in control. But in this way of working, the children have a lot of control.

This chapter will explore some of the ways in which the children at Fishergate exploit and enjoy their independence and control in this environment, but first of all it will focus on parental responses to risk-taking in the setting.

Parental responses to risk-taking

Previous chapters have already reported on a number of vignettes where children were making meaning from the open-ended play materials, sometimes with adult support and sometimes alone or with peers. The outdoor area is unusual in comparison with other early years' spaces but it seems the parents do quite quickly see that overall it is safe and, in addition, it is an interesting space for their children to be within. The following observation is illustrative of one parent's experience as she seems to observe both the implications of the activity for the safety of her son and the deep interests of the two reception boys.

Charley and Aroon sustained this activity outdoors, on an icy day, for almost an hour, as they moved from exploration of the materials to the combining of experimentation with an imaginative play scenario. However, we would argue that their final play scenario captured on film – the ice-machine – is much more than 'imaginative play'. They are making symbolic meaning of their world in the way that Worthington (2010b: 184) describes with 'imagination as dynamic change that supports children's understanding and meaning making of popular culture, new technologies, media and sometimes magic'. She draws on Van Oers's (2005: 8) work; he talks of imagination as abstract thinking and also speaks of imagination as a way of generating alternatives and of coming to understand how symbolic activity (imagination) connects with real-world experiences. In these terms, imagination is recognised as a complex cognitive process of which young children show themselves to be constantly capable.

Vignette 9

A visiting parent was outdoors with her son, who was exploring the outdoor area. It was winter and icy, and Charley and Aroon had brought out a plastic bottle, cut in half, containing frozen water, which the student teacher (Malcolm) had prepared and brought in for their work around water and ice. They were trying to free the ice from the bottle. They had put the bottle under their coats to 'warm it up' but this was cold and uncomfortable, they discovered, and Charley said 'It will be slow.' They were searching for faster methods and decided on force. They began throwing the bottle in the air so it would smash to the floor. They did this a few times and Aroon threw it behind his head, not knowing where it would land and laughing at Charley as he did so. They had edged closer to the visiting child and the mother was watching, noting that the bottle landed a few feet from where her son was playing.

Andy had also been watching and suggested to the boys that they came to another part of the playground and throw the bottle at a low wall to carry on their experiment. This they did and gradually lumps of ice began to leave the bottle. The ice was coloured and the pieces then became part of their ongoing play as they constructed an ice machine from available materials and then throwing the broken ice in a barrel and pouring in water 'to make ice for later'. 'We can come back tomorrow.' The visiting parent watched some of the ongoing play with the ice machine and was clearly interested in the progress of Charley's and Aroon's play as two other boys came to join them in the play scenario.

Although Pat did not speak to the parent on this occasion, there were other occasions when she did have conversations with parents in the outdoor area; these follow on. Before that, it is worth looking at Elizabeth's reflection during interview. Her general comment at this time illustrates how common the above scenario might be in this setting, with visiting parents, and how the team have now developed an awareness about how parents might feel and about how they can be prepared to respond to these potential feelings:

I think sometimes you can see some parents panicking. It's their precious child. You can see them thinking when some of the older lads are doing something a bit adventurous and they might be thinking: 'Gosh, my child's going to be in the midst of that'. But you can reassure them.

Here, the parental concerns around risk are not dismissed but are acknowledged as something that can be addressed through conversation and engagement with parents. Other visiting parents reflected with Pat when she asked them about their feelings of the outdoor area. She would explain who she was and what she was doing in the unit and then during the conversation ask for their impressions on the outdoor space. These were some of their responses, over time:

> You can see how these children are learning as they play. It takes away the stress that more formal settings can bring.
>
> I told my sister-in-law about this place and she cringes because her daughter is in a very formal class and I see the tension there for all of them.
>
> It surprised me that they're allowed to do it as most public institutions these days are so risk averse. So I was surprised they got permission. But I like it. Cole is very comfortable here. He has the space to look around. He's not always too happy being asked to conform although he can do it. But here he can explore and I just watch.
>
> When I first saw it, I thought, well this is different. It looks like a pile of junk. But this is our third visit and he loves it. He likes finding out what he can do and loves to be outdoors. He likes to paint and stick as well. He went to playgroup and was fine outside but didn't like it when they had to go in and be told.
>
> At first I thought some of the wood looked dangerous and was a bit tatty. And then I thought what if they pile the crates up and fall off but I've never seen anyone get hurt. They all seem to keep safe.

These parents must come to feel secure with the outdoor environment, otherwise it is doubtful that they would leave their child in the unit. No one to whom Pat spoke gave any indication of concerns about the outdoor area, over and above initial concerns on first visiting, as with the final comment above. Andy reported that one father had called the outdoor area 'the laboratory, because they're always experimenting'. Andy also reported that a look at the accident book shows that there are no more accidents in the outdoor space as it is now than there were with the more traditional bikes, scooters and climbing frames available on a daily basis.

The next section will look more closely at some apparent risk-taking enterprises from the children and then explore in a little more depth the ways in which adults are also taking risks in this open-ended play environment.

Children taking risks

It would be an oversimplification to say that the following play is 'typical' of what is often seen outdoors at Fishergate. Although children – both boys and girls – make bridges, ramps and slides on a regular basis, vignette 10 is unique in that it happened in exactly this way only once. Whereas the scenarios may have similar play themes within them, the actual activities are invariably unique because individual children bring the interests and preoccupations of the moment to the play activities and to the unfolding of the activities in collaboration with peers. The emerging play themes then reflect their intellectual preoccupations.

Vignette 10

Risky play: bridges, slides and tubes

Reflecting on risky play

Marco drags a long plank of wood over to the low wall and props one end against the wall, announcing: 'It's a slide.' Three other boys are in a different part of this area. He calls them and they come over to try the slide.

Jason comes over and looks at it and says: 'it's a bridge; it's a bridge.' Jason fetches more wood, saying: 'I know, let's make a bridge.' He selects a long thin piece and 'bridges' the gap in the wall where children enter and leave the enclosed play area. The plank is about one and a half metres long and just a few inches wide.

A new idea seems to be emerging for Jason: a bridge. He quickly enacts it in an appropriate gap in the wall; his concept of 'bridge' is well developed, it seems.

He tests the bridge, which bears his weight. Alistair comes to the bridge and says 'What is this thing?' He begins to walk across but Jason asks him to 'Stop. Go back. Let's fix it first. We're fixing it; we're fixing it.' Alistair retreats, watches and waits. Jason and Marco continue to add pieces of wood to the bridge, using some that Jason has brought.

This 'testing' requires very careful balancing, using his arms. It's not clear why Jason is stopping Alistair – does he think it is dangerous? Alistair clearly trusts his judgement and responds happily to Jason.

They prop the planks at almost 90 degrees to the bridge with pieces sticking up; these have to be stepped over as the narrow bridge is being crossed. Having made crossing the bridge more of a challenge, Jason and Marco try it out. Alistair returns and asks: 'How do I get up?' Jason points to the low wall and then to the bridge: 'There, there and there.'

So, 'fixing the bridge' means increasing the challenge, not making it safer.

Alistair seems to understand that Jason knows what to do; Jason is his main reference point in meeting the challenge.

Alistair does as suggested, putting his feet where Jason points, but the crossing seems quite a challenge for Alistair. He wobbles and

Alistair is pleased at his success.

moves quite slowly but succeeds: 'I did it, I did it.'

He goes to the slide and asks Jason: 'Is it slippy?' He says: 'No.' Alistair talks about the time he went down 'one like this, and I fell and it hurt'. He looks at it again and goes down the slide in a low crouch. Others come to test the challenging bridge and seem quite confident.

Jason takes an interest whilst Alistair relives his previous experience and related anxieties; Jason seems to take Alistair's concerns seriously. No one makes fun of Alistair despite their obvious skills.

One boy crawls through a long tube over by the wall; as he emerges, he calls: 'Look at me.' The others laugh and one shouts: 'He's the very hungry caterpillar.' Several other children follow him through the tube. One child looks inside but does not go through although he watches the other children do so.

The link with the familiar story seems to generate heightened interest in the children; perhaps they relive the story in their minds as they crawl through the tube. The child who chooses not to go may not know the story or may feel it remains too scary at this time to commit to the journey

---

EYFS learning outcomes

KUW: Investigate objects and materials by using all the senses as appropriate.

KUW: Build and construct with a wide range of objects, selecting appropriate resources and adapting their work where necessary.

PD: Show understanding of the need for safety when tackling new challenges. Construct with large materials such as cartons, fabric and planks.

PD: Practise some appropriate safety measures without direct supervision.

There were no adults involved at any time in the play, although there were adults in the outdoor area with the children and Andy commented afterwards on the new skills that some of the boys were exhibiting in the play. The children's individual journals which record play and learning, the conversations with the team and several of the filmed sequences all show that this type of play is a continuing favourite with this group of boys; there are many variations on this theme of building in the outdoor area; using planks and bridges occur and recur with regularity for these boys and for other children. Here the boys take risks as they cross the bridge; it is not an easy task for them. Crawling through the pipe also takes courage; it is a long enclosed space with no real guarantee that exit can be achieved, although children will have seen other children crawling through it and emerging successfully to repeat the crawl many times but each child needs to understand this before they take the risk. In this play, the children do not seem to take risks without calculating the risks they are taking. Recall vignette 3 in Chapter 2, when a group of children built and used the assault course around the playground, and the ways in which different children responded in their own ways to the evident risks. As we watched this play on screen we agreed that this kind of play that included the making of ramps as well as bridges on a regular basis was not in fact repetitive play; rather it was the same experiment being conducted under different conditions and with different and more sophisticated outcomes for children, including the designing of greater risks whilst playing.

Roxanna, whose mother was in the armed forces, was a prominent person in the initial design of the assault course. In this next vignette, we return again to Roxanna, playing with Edward and Sadie, with whom she often plays. One point of particular interest in vignette 11 is that the older children (Edward, Roxanna and Sadie) are taking risks that they are clearly comfortable with. This seems to be a familiar activity for them although Edward does choose to self-exclude at one point and observes the two girls. Alongside them is Robbie, three years old and relatively new to the setting, not connected to their play but happily engaged in exploring the resources. He often drags a piece of wood, a sweeping brush or a plastic pipe around the playground – a potential hazard for others but no one ever seems to fall over them. However, Robbie also stands and watches their play with considerable interest and seems to want to try it out for himself once the group of players has moved away.

Vignette 11

Rope swinging

Edward, Roxanna and Sadie are swinging on a rope secured to the wall in two places (see Figure 5.1). It spans a pile of tyres and rope and they swing backwards and forwards,

Reflecting on the play

Roxanna seems to enjoy physical play, as does Sadie; they do a lot of design activities indoors and outdoors. It may be that these opportunities

Figure 5.1 Tyres and ropes make a place for swinging.

their bodies at full stretch. First Sadie and then Roxanna climbs the outer side of the steps into school; this is a narrow ledge and quite high from the floor, requiring each girl to hold onto the outer side of the railings to avoid falling off. Roxanna moves across onto the rope at its highest point and swings down onto the tyres below. Sadie watches but does not follow on this occasion.

Sadie goes to Robbie, who is standing close to them with a long piece of wood. She takes it from him, speaking inaudibly and returns it to the wood pile. He watches her but says nothing. She returns, puts her hands on her hips and shakes her head at him. He moves away.

for risky play in this environment allows girls additional time to break out of their stereotypes to be physical, to design, to take calculated risks. Andy comments that Edward has had a long friendship with Roxanna and Sadie has joined them later.

It is not possible to hear what Sadie is saying to Robbie but she clearly sees some kind of threat – real or imagined – from him at this point. Robbie does not seem worried about her intervention.

The three children return to the rope and swing on it but Edward moves away and watches. The two girls go on and swing in unison, very widely and very vigorously backwards and forwards; their bodies are at full stretch but their legs are well positioned to brace themselves. After three attempts to catch the rope, Edward joins them. This continues and Robbie returns to their 'orbit', dragging a sweeping brush. They look but ignore him.

The three of them then cross the playground to a pile of tubes and tubing. They have to balance to cross this to climb over the wall into the enclosed area. Here they begin to play at magic potions together. Later, when the primary children come out to play, they return to the rope and tyres and climb there and Roxanna once again climbs the sides of the steps to chat to some of the older children.

Meanwhile, as they leave to play at magic potions, Robbie has gone to the tyres and ropes that they have abandoned and is trying to swing on the rope while standing on the tyres as they did. He is having problems keeping his balance. He then begins to investigate the inside of a tyre, laying across it and running his hand around the inner rim several times and very carefully.

He then moves to the lowest point of the rope to stand on a tyre and hold onto the rope. Because there are fewer tyres here, it is more stable and he begins to carefully edge his way higher the rope, holding on carefully and moving very slowly until he chooses to go no further.

This may be a familiar activity; it seems to be carefully and knowingly choreographed by the two girls to provide them with the maximum thrill and challenge.

They could have entered through an opening but following Roxanna's lead seem to choose the most physically challenging way to enter the enclosed area.

Robbie's previous observations have clearly been purposeful. He wants to try the challenge but is smaller and less skilled at this stage of his development. He incorporates the close investigation of the inside of the tyre.

It is almost as if the tyre investigation gave Robbie some time to rethink his engagement with the rope and to achieve his goal of swinging, albeit minimally and carefully; his face shows pleasure at his goal achievement.

EYFS learning outcomes

KUW: Investigate objects and materials by using all their senses as appropriate.

KUW: Find out about their environment and talk about those features they like and dislike.

PD: Move with confidence, imagination and safety.

PD: Show understanding of the need for safety when tackling new challenges.

Little and Wyver (2010) report their research with four- and five-year-olds relating to risk-taking in outdoor environments. They conclude that children of this age are capable of making risk judgements and do use these judgements when playing with outdoor equipment. Children show a good level of awareness of understanding a relationship between their capabilities, their behaviour and potential injury outcomes. Stephenson (2003) shows also how two- and three-year-olds will put themselves in positions of risk-taking although they are more likely to need adults to help them surmount the risks once engaged with than are older children. Nevertheless, risk assessment, risk-taking and overcoming risks within the environment would seem to be an essential part of the path to maturity and self reliance, and being adventurous and taking risks are useful dispositions in thinking and problem-solving (Costa 1991; Tishman *et al.* 1993), as we have seen in each of the above vignettes.

Educators intervening in risk-taking

In vignette 9, earlier in this chapter, we saw Andy's intervention in the plastic bottle throwing that Charley and Aroon were engaged with. He was sensitive to their experimentation because he had been observing it; the team were using the icy weather to extend the children's spontaneous interests in water and ice and the student was gaining experience in initiating some planned activities that children might choose to take forward in their own ways. Charley and Aroon had clearly grasped the concept of melting and were experimenting with their own capacity to speed up the process. Andy intervened by allowing them to sustain the experimental nature of their activity whilst also recognising the visiting mother's concern and, indeed, the potential risk of throwing heavy plastic bottles in undirected ways. This next vignette offers a chance to reflect on a less well planned intervention by Pat, who interacted with a boy in a spontaneous and well-intended way but, on reflection, came to see that it really could have been managed much more effectively. Interestingly, in terms of risk-taking, it is very similar to the previous vignette in terms of children stretching their bodies to an extreme.

Vignette 12

Pat was in conversation with a visitor in the outdoor area and was not filming at this point. Suddenly, she heard a shout that suggested distress and looked towards the wooden fence that separated the outdoor area from the wider school playground. Three boys, all four-year-olds, were each standing on the sloping centre of a large cable reel, balanced on their outer rims. They were each at full stretch and holding on to the top of the fence. One boy's reel was rolling away from the fence and he was holding on grimly, clearly very close to being pulled away from the fence and falling heavily onto the tarmac. He called again. Pat ran across and put her hands under his armpits and lifted him down onto his feet. The boy was clearly angry with Pat and 'slapped' her arm firmly but not intending to hurt her. Pat apologised, saying: 'I'm sorry; I could see you were falling.' The boy turned away, pushed the cable reel closer to the fence and climbed up again to join his two peers, laughing at them and once again taking up his risky balanced position on the perilous cable reel.

What Pat realised was that she should have gently rolled the cable reel back against the wall to allow the boy to regain his footing, without any further intervention on her part. The boy was angry because he felt humiliated; an adult had lifted him 'like a baby' down from his reel, whereas the enterprise was designed to make him feel competent and skilled in a risky environment and to test his courage to its limits along with his friends as co-players in this risky enterprise.

Educators as pedagogic risk-takers

In this next vignette, the boys playing together are older boys in the unit. They are familiar with one another and have an extensive shared history of exploring their outdoor environment and of directing their play in independent, self-determined ways. Here, we can see high levels of cooperation and joint goal-setting. Because this has been captured on film, it is possible to watch the sequences again and again. This gives opportunities to reflect on the children's play in deeper and deeper ways, to make meaning where none might seem to be, if we were to pass by and to see this happening in real time. Some might interpret this play as low level; these boys appear, at first glance, to be pouring water on powder paint and making rather a large 'mess' in the outdoor area. It might be recalled that, in Chapter 4, staff talked about visitors to the unit 'not always getting it'. This could also be such an occasion, when someone not familiar with the long-term achievements of children might see this episode as pointless time-wasting.

Herein lies the inherent risks for the early years team. When they look at children's play, they have learned to look for and then to see purpose, just as repeated viewing of this play allowed Andy and Pat to begin to see shared purpose across the children's individual actions. However, others may see only 'chaos and mess' and in so doing may also come to doubt the educational integrity of adults who allow these instances to continue uninterrupted and with seemingly no adult intervention of any kind. It is not always possible to observe the whole of children's play; this forthcoming play continued over a period of about 75 minutes. The filming captured only parts of it but putting these extracts together gives a clearer insight into the continuity and progression in the play, the purpose and intent, the design and goal orientation of these cooperatively engaged peers.

It has been previously noted that water themes are prevalent in the play at Fishergate, in a city where the River Ouse is a constant and substantial presence for the children. Here we see Zack again, who made a boat at the woodwork bench (vignette 7, Chapter 4).

Vignette 13

Making a river	Why is this activity a valuable learning experience? Why is it risky for adults?
Zack and Marco have been using the outdoor powder paints to paint the playground. They use blue, then orange, then green, and are talking as they work. Someone pours water on the paint and the play has developed into a 'river' as there is a slight incline. Marco moves some water around with a piece of paper; he seems to be carefully mixing water with the colours and watching the changes. Zack remarks 'It's a rainbow' as he paints. Jason drips water slowly onto the 'painting' from a salt container.	Sometimes, the adults initiate outdoor painting activities. The children are also allowed to paint on the lower windows of the unit; the rationale is: 'It's powder paint, it washes off.' Recall the time when Andy used the internet to find crate and tyre sculptures; the team are seeking to promote a sense of responsibility for creative activities on a large scale.

Zack and Marco seem to find all these developments quite acceptable and ask for more water to be fetched. Robbie comes over and stirs the water/river with his long piece of wood watching the colours mix; the others are aware of him but do not speak to him, nor do they stop him. Robbie has been playing with this piece of wood for much of the morning; he is often seen passing in front of the camera on his travels as he trails it behind. It is also the piece of wood Sadie took from him in vignette 11 in this chapter.

Jason notices that the water/river has gone under the fence into the bigger playground. He calls to the others to look and points. Zack fetches more water, as does Alistair; Jason throws his container down and fetches something bigger; the salt container goes under the fence to the larger playground. Robbie opens the gate and goes through to fetch the container, returns and closes the gate behind him. He throws the container back towards the boys, who are now adding paint to the water. He returns a little later to jump over the 'river' twice.

Marco and Zack are painting the floor and chatting. Alistair brings more water and pours it on. He runs to the fence to see where the river is and calls the others over, shouting: 'Look. Look, it's longer.' Zack returns to paint and, as Jason comes out with more water, Zack calls: 'Put it on the paint, on the paint.' Jason complies. Robbie is back, running his wood through the water. He is ignored. Zack calls out: 'It's the rainbow river.'

The children show a well-developed sense of 'the creative process' as iterative: building over time, with each action linked to the next. They show real interest in the properties of paint and water; they are studying intently, with deep concentration, as again is Robbie (as in vignette 11 when he watched the children swinging on the pulley).

There is a strong sense of discovery here: what happens when more water is added to the 'river'. They are autonomously collaborative, including Robbie, who seems to understand their goals although he remains generally peripheral to the main activity.

As Andy watches this play, he comments that this is a good example of letting the play go as far as it needs to. He acknowledges that some adults might not allow this but believes these children are absorbed and are exploring new ideas.

EYFS learning outcomes

CLL: Interact with others, negotiating plans and activities and taking turns in conversation.

CLL: Enjoy listening to and using spoken and written language, and readily turn to it in their play and learning.

CLL: Use talk to organise, sequence and clarify thinking, ideas, feelings and events.

PSRN: Use everyday words to describe position.

This next vignette shows adult intervention in play and perhaps gives us some indication of from where Zack and his friends in vignette 13 get their ideas or indeed understand that they have permission to 'paint the playground'. In fact not only is Andy intervening in this forthcoming play, he has initiated it with Rebecca, who is a relatively new girl in the unit, and with Owen, who is much older than Rebecca but has not established any strong friendships in the unit. During this particular period, Owen was often captured on film as a solitary player. However, as with vignette 13, it may be that those adults who 'don't get it' might wonder why Andy engages as he does with Owen and Rebecca. Debbie is also present; she is recording some of their activity on camera as well as interacting with the activity.

Vignette 14

Powder paint play outside

Andy's reflections and intentions

Andy has laid a long sheet of paper on the floor outside and taken out the large containers of powder paint. Rebecca and Owen are wearing all-in-one waterproof suits and wellingtons. As the camera picks them up there is blue paint on the paper and Rebecca is walking though it and jumping into it. Debbie is heard calling: 'Oh, running and jumping. good one.' Rebecca claps her hands. Debbie

This was a planned experience based on previous observations of Rebecca and Owen as they had explored the properties of mud and water by splashing in puddles. What was fascinating was the way in which this activity brought these children together socially. Owen engaged with the asks Owen:'Do you want a different colour?' He nods. Debbie asks: 'What other colours did you bring, Mr Burt?' Andy and Owen go to look. Debbie asks:'Are you going to try all the colours?' Owen answers excitedly: 'Mr Burt, we need to try all the colours, we need to try all the colours.' Owen dips a container into the powder paint and throws it onto the blue. Rebecca also does this. Owen comes back for more; Andy states 'I think you have plenty, let's see how you get on with that' but allows Owen to dip his container in again and get some more yellow, which he throws on. Owen jumps into the powder and it flies upwards, some paint going on Rebecca's covered legs. Owen and Rebecca laugh. Debbie remarks to Andy: 'He seems to be enjoying the getting dirty part now, doesn't he? I've noticed that in the last few weeks.' Andy is saying 'Wow, look at that' as Owen moves around the paper and Rebecca watches him. Owen asks for some white and Debbie opens it up for him. Rebecca is jumping in the powder paint and Owen brings his white over. He throws it on and moves the powder around with his feet, then calls out: 'It's green, it's gone green. Makes green. Look at that green.'

activity and with Rebecca and with myself and Debbie in ways that had not been observed before. It is hard to imagine Owen being as engaged as he is here, outdoors, with a directed, table-based, colour-mixing activity that might happen indoors. It certainly seems that the more physical aspect and larger scale of the outdoors helps him to express his ideas and feelings comfortably. Also, although this was an adult-planned activity, it is the children who take the lead as they explore. Planning in this way is significant in signalling a more balanced relationship between the children and adults; a relationship which enables these perhaps unorthodox yet highly creative activities to take place.

At Fishergate then, both the children and the adults take risks of one kind or another – each of them acting in the pursuit of new knowledge and understandings. The next section now takes a look at aspects of conflict and conflict resolution by the children.

Conflict

The value of conflict

Conflict occurs throughout life and in all social contexts. Where more than one human is gathered, then at some point, conflict and its resolution, or lack of resolution, will feature in the discourse. Conflict can take many forms in adults; adults learn the sophistications of conflict through angry silence and through inaction, along with the more overt expressions of conflict with loved ones, colleagues and, occasionally, strangers – think of road rage, queue rage and so on. Conflict is inevitable in life for all ages and at different levels of expression. Part of the growth to maturity involves the capacity to contain rage, as a common feature of conflict, to express strong emotions in appropriate ways and of course to utilise strategies for resolving conflict when it arises in day-to-day interactions. Individuals without the capacity for conflict resolution are individuals who quickly become out of control and, through this loss of control, perhaps do physical and emotional damage to themselves and to others.

This is no different for children. As Hedegaard (2008: 23) points out, conflicts can occur between infants and parents establishing day and night rhythms, in relation to breast-feeding and, later, in developing eating patterns. This happens because the child is beginning to develop competences associated with autonomy. It becomes a problem for child and parent when the adult 'cannot see the child's perspective or cannot see the child's motive' (Hedegaard 2008: 24). Young children have both perspective and motive; their actions are purposeful and of course a key part of their early experience and development is to have that purpose shaped by the social and cultural norms of the family in which they live and, as they become older, the institutions they attend, which are of course themselves culturally shaped by the adults who work in them.

Different societies evolve many similar and some different ways of dealing with conflict. These are 'culturally patterned choices' (Fry 2000: 334) and can be both formal – such as drawing on a central authority figure to mediate the conflict – and informal – such as agreeing to share a high-status object. An individual's repertoire for conflict resolution grows as he/she becomes more exposed to the strategies in common usage in the communities with which he/she engages. Of course, for children in an early years setting, these community reference points are home and school, and the 'culturally patterned choices' of the two locations may themselves be similar or different, or in fact both at times. We are not suggesting that one culture is automatically right and one is wrong; the important point is, as Hedegaard suggests above, understanding the child's perspective and motive without making uninformed generalisations about home experiences necessarily being 'worse' than school experiences. What research does show is that children who are developing in environments where conflict resolution strategies are modelled and discussed by adults are more likely to adopt these techniques as cultural norms (Aureli and de Waal 2000). Also, as children become older, they are increasingly able to make peace after conflict if opportunities present themselves (Butovskaya et al. 2000). It appears at an earlier age in cultures that value cooperation and kinship. It has also been shown (Broadhead 2009: 115) that what may at first appear to be 'misbehaviour, chaos and conflict' can often act, through self-initiated reconciliation, as a platform for the play to become more complex and intellectually challenging.

We hope that the following examples of conflict and conflict resolution as filmed at Fishergate can help to expand understanding about the relationship between the provision of open-ended play spaces in educational settings and the way in which children subsequently use these spaces to explore and resolve conflict, build relationships and begin to form important friendships.

Conflict resolution at Fishergate

It should be stated at the outset that there were few instances of conflict captured on film because there are few such instances in the setting. We have already seen some of these in vignette 2, Chapter 2, when Sebastian entered Archie's and Luke's design and then returned to throw a plank, in vignette 3 with some pushing on the assault course, and then in vignette 6, Chapter 3, with the five girls and their lizards. Although captured on film, none of these incidents drew the attention of other adults; they were all resolved by the children and at no time did play cease because of the developing conflicts. Conflicts may occur more frequently when the children are new, and exploring the space and its resources and getting to know one another. As Verbeek and colleagues (2000: 34) point out, objects often become desired as soon as another child picks them up and 'this conflict may serve to test the social waters'. However, in the outdoor area at Fishergate, there are so many open-ended resources that children seem to learn very quickly that there is plenty for everyone.

Throughout the time of filming, there were children in the unit with learning delay and developmental delay, or children who as yet had little English who were operating at a lower level of sociability than would be usual and as a consequence might be more inclined to become impatient or angry when frustrated, as we saw with Sebastian when he threw the plank. However, Andy commented often on the fact that the open-ended approach to activity and resource provision seemed to imbue the setting with less potential for conflict for all children. Debbie remarked similarly when reflecting on the old way of working and the move to more open-endedness in provision:

> Children's behaviour is fantastic now; we don't have many problems, the odd bickering maybe. But before, when we were asking them to do what we wanted them to do all the time, we had more behaviour issues, whereas now, we don't.

In order to further explore issues around conflict resolution, we have selected two pieces of film that involve the same three boys, Cole, Joe and Tobias. Andy had noted that Joe and Tobias have recently established a close friendship with one another and are choosing to play together more frequently. Tobias had been in the setting for about a year and Joe for just over a term; both attend full-time and are quite close in age as five-year-olds. Cole is a full-time reception child but has not yet established any particular friendships. He is often involved in small conflicts; his social skills are not yet well developed and it may be that he sees conflict-related initiations as culturally normal. He does seem to provoke them on a regular but not frequent basis.

In these two vignettes, Joe and Tobias reveal a range of strategies for managing Cole and Cole is clearly showing interest in, and perhaps a desire to engage with, the two boys in their design-related activities outdoors. As Andy and Pat watched the films, we wondered if Cole returned to Joe and Tobias because they seemed to have high levels of tolerance for his behaviour, although they are clearly not always pleased with it. Much of the time, the filming has not captured the conversations between the boys because Pat was too far away; she was concerned that too close a proximity would influence the interaction. Interestingly, both vignettes also show high levels of risk-taking by the three boys.

Vignette 15

Initiating and managing conflict

Reflections on purpose and meaning

Joe and Tobias have gone over to the bread crates, piled about five high in four stacks. Joe climbs confidently up onto the stacks and begins to move along the top of the stacks, holding onto the wooden fence that they are stacked beside, in a crouching position. Tobias is throwing crates onto the floor and then he goes around a crate while Joe climbs down from a high crate. They run around the outdoor area a few times with Tobias following Joe.

About 15 minutes later they return to the crates and watch Billy as he pours water down the slide. Joe is sitting high up on the crates and they are chatting as they watch. Tobias stands on the floor. They stay for several minutes and seem to be thinking and talking. Billy comes and goes with water in a watering can to pour down the slide. Joe is staring, very still. Tobias leaves but Joe stays, sitting and watching and thinking, perhaps.

Is Tobias concerned that the crates are piled too high for him so he is reducing the risk as he sees it? Joe seems not to interpret Tobias's 'throwing of crates' as he later does when Cole does it. He seems to differentiate the purpose each boy has for doing it: Tobias for 'safety', Cole for 'destruction', perhaps?

Andy wondered if Joe was day-dreaming and recalled a children's author speaking on television of the importance of allowing children to daydream in school. We have commented several times in vignettes on these thinking modes that children adopt, often, as does Joe here, for quite long periods.

Later on Tobias and Joe are in the area and Cole runs outside and joins them. Joe and Tobias have built a barrier across crates – Joe says to Cole: 'You can use a password if you want to get past here.' Cole throws a hoop on the floor; Joe says to Tobias: 'Look what Cole just did'. Cole smiles. They speak to him. Cole kicks crates down and Joe speaks to him but it is inaudible. Cole watches as Joe rebuilds. Joe seems to be leading the design. Andy joins them and they talk about this being their ship. Andy leaves the area. Cole stands on one crate and kicks another down. He throws down a bread crate, lifts another and climbs on it, looking always at Joe. Cole and Joe are balancing.

Although Cole has been in the setting for almost a year, Andy feels he is only just coming to understand what resources there are and what he might do with them. He thinks Cole is trying to get a reaction from Joe, that he wants an interaction but has no other means of initiating it.

Joe then goes inside; Cole follows and then comes out again as if looking for Joe. He goes to the area where they were playing; Joe has returned. Cole enters the area and uses the entrance as it should be used, chats to Joe and then kicks several crates around. Joe watches and carries on with his play.

Joe does keep returning to a proximity to Cole despite his occasional 'destructive' outbursts. He does not go to find an adult to manage Cole. By using the entrance correctly, Cole demonstrates that he understands that rules do apply and that he can comply when he wishes.

EYFS learning outcomes

It seems less useful to consider the EYFS outcomes and goals as they pertain to this episode because the children are exhibiting very different levels of 'being' in this instance. Joe and Tobias together made quite complex constructions for their play scenarios but Cole is exhibiting developmental elements of a much younger child in this play. Like Sebastian in vignette 2, Chapter 2, Cole does not seem to understand the contextual frame for the play, nor does he seem able or willing to watch the play; at least this is not captured on film.

Further reflection suggests that Cole seems to be more interested in Joe's responses to him than in Tobias's, and indeed Tobias seems uninterested in Cole. Sometimes Joe looks puzzled by Cole; he remonstrates with him and does occasionally ask him: 'Why did you do that?' Although Cole is clearly intent on throwing the resources around at times, the conflict never escalates, perhaps because Joe has learned how to take a reasoned response and is demonstrating that here, or perhaps because Cole really is exercising some control.

This next vignette, between the same three boys, took place a few days later. The three-way link seems much the same and the roles they take are also much the same. However, Joe does seek adult help here and seems angrier than in the previous encounter, whereas Tobias seems far more confident in his climbing. Cole does not speak throughout the encounter but he is highly watchful, more so than in vignette 15. He seems to have decided that it is Joe with whom he wants to interact, as he makes no attempt to move Tobias from his position in the crates after the initial attempt to take his milk crate. Perhaps he finds Tobias more assertive than Joe; perhaps it is Joe whom he wants for a friend.

Vignette 16

The three boys are together on stacked bread crates in the outside area. Tobias pulls a milk crate onto the stacked bread crates; Cole attempts to remove it but Tobias shouts 'Cole' angrily and glares, and Cole stops. Tobias manoeuvres the crate and sits high on top to watch the older children at their playtime; he looks precarious but seems intent on getting comfortable. Joe is sitting in a bread crate and looks comfortable, having more room; he climbs out and Cole climbs into the bread crate and lies down. Joe watches him. Tobias climbs down, points to the milk crate he has been sitting on, shouts 'Take that out for me, this is not very, very good' and runs off to get a larger bread crate from a pile to replace his smaller milk crate. Joe pushes out the milk crate; Tobias piles in the more suitable bread crate and gets comfortable to resume watching the older children at play. Cole has sat up and is watching Joe and Tobias. Joe goes and gets another bread crate and slides it in next to Tobias. Cole moves across to take possession of Joe's two bread crates and Joe is angry: 'No, Cole has taken my thing.' He stamps away and stands against the wall, glowering at Cole. Tobias and Cole watch him and he returns. Cole lies down across both bread crates, making it clear that he is stopping Joe from returning to the 'perch'. Joe shouts at Cole 'I am going to tell' and walks off. Cole sits up and watches and moves aside as Joe returns with Andy. Andy says 'Well, I think there is space still' and stays for a few moments in discussion. Cole has moved over and Joe attempts to climb in but the structure is now too high with the third bread crate. Joe fetches milk crates to stand on but this is wobbly so he fetches a cable reel which allows him to climb over the edge and into the bread crate and sit between Tobias and Cole. Cole has not tried to take over the bread crate again whilst Joe is climbing. Tobias and Joe are chatting and watching the older children as they play in the primary school playground. Cole lays down again as Joe climbs out and Tobias says 'Oh oh. Get off', pushing at Cole's feet. Joe seems not to care and walks away. He returns and climbs in again, using the cable reel. Cole is still lying down but there seems to be room for both of them, Joe seated and Cole lying down, watching Joe. Cole wriggles and pushes and Joe climbs out again and dances around. Filming stops here.

This chapter has aimed to show how risk-taking, conflict and conflict resolution might be perceived as normal and educative aspects of life in the early years; how they might flow and benefit children without, necessarily, any direct adult intervention as distinct from adult awareness. The early years team were aware of Cole's lack of social skills and did monitor his interactions. We have also included reference to risk-taking as a pedagogical activity whereby adults might engage in activities from which other adults may seem unable to glean purpose. So how do these two dimensions – conflict and risk – link to our model for open-ended play (Table 0.1)?

Risk-taking and conflict resolution are presented here as integral aspects of what some children choose to be or do at certain times in their early years settings, for a whole range of reasons, many of which we may never know – indeed what many will continue to do throughout their lives. If these are normal parts of their experiential need, then adults have some responsibility, pedagogically, for creating environments in which they can find both expression and resolution. Although we (and others) do suggest that adults have a responsibility to encourage calculated risk, we are not prompting the encouragement of conflict. We are saying that conflict is an inevitable part of human contact and hope we have demonstrated in this chapter and in others that, where conflict has been described, there are links between young children's capacities to exhibit and develop conflict resolution strategies and the early years environments in which they find themselves. Access to open-ended resources seems to have links with conflict resolution and also with creating and sustaining an environment where the inevitability of conflict does not detract from or diminish positive learning experiences; indeed it may become an integral part of them.

Chapter 6 goes on to take a look at the longitudinal development of four

Table 0.1 Playful pedagogies and playful learning: the juxtaposition model

'Open-ended play': understanding playful pedagogies	'The whatever you want it to be place': revealing playful learning
A way for the adult to conceive of her/ his own role in creating and sustaining an educational environment that is flexible enough to allow children's interests and experiences to emerge and develop; it also encompasses the adults' responsibilities in identifying, recording and planning for those interests in systematic but flexible ways and a responsibility to look for ways of extending those interests and relating them to the wider world in which the child is living and learning.　　The early years setting becomes a space and place where adults nurture potential and push the boundaries of their personal understandings of playful learning and playful pedagogies.	The environment and its possibilities as perceived and engaged with from the child's perspective. The child enters a space where anything is possible – whether a large or small space – and where they can engage alone or with others in exploring and exploiting that environment to match the images, plans and memories that emerge from their own minds, experiences and skills.　　The early years setting becomes a space and place where children explore their identity, potential and interests and push back the boundaries of personal possibility through playful engagement.

children at Fishergate, to explore and consider how their individual increasing expertise in accessing their open-ended play environment adds to their progression as learners as they make these spaces their own.

From the 'new child' to the 'master player'

Playful progression from child-initiated activities

What do we mean by 'master players'?

Reynolds and Jones (1997) present and explore the concept of the 'master player' to consider the complexity of children's play and the nature of the adult's role in supporting the journey towards mastery. They state (p. 11):

> The young master player is competent because she is playing. Time for play is valuable because play is the child's most comfortable medium – in play the child is sharp. Because 4 and 5 year olds are at their best when they are playing, it is the mode that allows them to practise other skills: taking initiative and solving problems within the constraints of tasks or rules, focussing attention for long periods of time, negotiating social relationships, inventing and imposing patterns and order and manipulating materials and ideas in creative ways.

We hope the previous chapters have gone some way to illustrating the detail of this complexity in action in the detailed vignettes of children's play in the early years unit at Fishergate. However, in using the term 'master player', the book is not proposing that there is some state of comparative excellence that all children should reach; some 'level' of mastery that might be measured. Such a notion would be completely contrary to the fundamental principle of play: that it belongs to the player and does not exist to support comparative analyses of any kind. Both in Reynolds and Jones's (1997) work and in our own thinking, 'mastery' is a state that each child may attain for her/himself in the right kinds of play environments. It is an individualised state that can be recognised and acknowledged through observing and reflecting on children's play (just as the early years team do at Fishergate) and as Moyles and colleagues discuss (Moyles 2010) in proposing a reflective approach to understanding the complexities of play and its provision for early years educators. The claim in this book is that, in the right kind of playfully structured, educational environment, all children can make progress; all children can claim some degree of mastery over the necessary skills of play and engagement – and there are many skills to be mastered, as the analyses of the vignettes have shown; many more than are contained in the early learning outcomes and goals.

In particular, this book is focussing on mastery in 'open-ended play spaces' or, as taken from the child's perspective, 'the whatever you want it to be place'. We have tried to make specific links between the opportunities for free choice from a wide range of open-ended materials as stimulating the kinds of creative, problem-solving, high-concentration, cooperative engagements that Reynolds and Jones describe above. We are aiming to show how it is possible to create and sustain such spaces, along with the complexities and challenges of doing so, to allow all children to flourish in their development of mastery in play.

Over the months of data collection, Pat spent a considerable time filming and observing the children and early years team at Fishergate. As stated in the previous chapter, throughout that time there were few instances of conflict and very few, and always very low-key, instances of staff management of inappropriate behaviour. That is not to say that there were no children with special needs in the class, either through learning delay or with behavioural difficulties; there were such children and the team were aware of their needs but the children themselves were seldom prominent during day-to-day activities. Pat's written comments whilst in the setting one day show her own reflections on the links between the environment and the move towards mastery for all children, including those with special educational needs:

Pat's written reflections

S. with severe learning difficulties and a special needs statement now understands the 'empty hands' order at tidy up time and goes with the other children to the toilet and to wash her hands. Children with difficulties do need a key adult with them at times but they blend and learn as time goes on. We see other children understanding the need to care for them: 'I'll look after you S.' 'S can come with me'. They see her behaviour as different but seem to understand that 'different' can be accepted as 'the same' as time passes and as other adults model consistent and positive engagements with special children. But, in fact, as I watch, I can see that the adults' engagements with special children are no different from their engagements with other children. They may be more frequent and over time, the special children, although still special, seem more assimilated and able to do more of what the other children can do.

I think I see this more clearly because I visit intermittently. I see the development of their social and intellectual skills more evidently from visit to visit and I see their deeper engagement in activities as a clear progression from when last observed. I think I can understand the ways in which the environment has impacted on these developments in that the environment asks relatively little of the children in terms of complying with adult directives. This seems to be the key for them. Today, S. sat well at snack and received a smiley face. She sticks it on herself and understands this is a reward. She takes it off and sticks it on again and smiles. Her key adult gives her a smiley face for her doll. She walks around looking at the stickers and smiling.

The reader might recall the boat-building activity in Chapter 4 when Debbie worked with a group of girls to design and build. At one point, S. moves into this activity and begins to place bricks in random places. The girls make no comment and just move them as they need to. S. then locates bricks in the 'correct' places and at one point lies down within the boundaries of the emerging boat and goes 'to sleep'. The girls just work round her, careful not to hurt her. She moves in and out of the developing boat several times, not a part of the group but not rejected by the group either. She seems to enjoy the close proximity to others and there was no sense of the kinds of disruption of activities that had been evident in her early days at Fishergate; S. is achieving her own level of mastery. She too, like children younger than her at Fishergate, enjoys watching the play of more experienced players.

Later in this chapter, four case studies are presented, of progression in children who each, in their own way, became a master player at Fishergate over time. We have not selected children with statements of special educational needs because it would be impossible to protect their identities. However, we have selected three children who had some initial difficulties or challenges in settling into the unit.

Before we present the case studies, the next section explores a concept that Andy and Pat spent quite a bit of time discussing during joint research and reflection: how new children come to understand and 'map' the indoor and outdoor play areas at Fishergate. We came to see this ability to internally and geographically map both the indoor and outdoor spaces as key parts of becoming masterful in play.

Becoming familiar with the play environment: the first step towards mastery

It is probably the case that, as educators of young children, we often take for granted the huge amount of knowledge and understanding that young children have to gradually amass once they enter an early years environment for the first time. Previous vignettes have explored the children's design and use of 'doors' and this prompted reflection on their potential importance in children's lives. A door must represent the unknown to them as they move from the familiarity of their own homes, mapped over many months and years, and learn to map unfamiliar environments in the wider world. There must be many times when they experience the feeling of either not knowing or only partly knowing and remembering what is beyond a particular doorway. They take a great deal on trust of the adults around them, and clearly new children have yet to get to know and trust the adults and the other children in their setting. In addition, in the indoor area, many pieces of furniture create barriers for them at their head-height so, unlike the adults, they have no oversight of the whole space at one glance. This is not the case in the outdoor area, where they can scan the whole space as they wish.

Consider these two cameos and their interpretations, taken from observational notes as these two new children learn to understand the indoor and outdoor spaces at Fishergate.

Vignette 17: Melinda explores

Melinda explores

Reflecting on Melinda's explorations

Melinda is new in the setting and has been coming for about two weeks; she is an older three-year-old. She plays alone with the beads. She then lies down on an empty shelf and watches a boy jumping from his brick design onto the floor. She says to him: 'That's where boys sleep.' She calls him 'a baby' and smiles at him. They briefly interconnect their play as 'dogs laying down to sleep'. The boy leaves.

Melinda goes to the writing area and gets a piece of paper and begins to draw. A member of staff comes to sit with her and she says: 'I am making a picture for my mummy.' She talks also about her auntie and her granny.

She leaves the table and goes to watch the fish in the tank. She fetches a chair to stand on so she can get closer to them and observes them for some time. She goes to the computer and asks Pat 'Is it sick?' as it is turned off. Pat says she does not know because she is a visitor and to ask a teacher. Melinda returns and says to Pat 'It's sick'

Although she begins by playing alone, Melinda is taking an interest in what other children are doing and is confident enough to initiate a conversation and sustain a brief interaction. Children often lie on the shelves when the bricks have been removed; perhaps it is a safe, boundaried space to relax in.

Melinda is already learning where areas and materials are. She brings thoughts of home and family into the setting with her; perhaps she is thinking about them even as she explores her new environment, and this suggests she already feels relaxed here. When she sees pencil and paper she already knows what to do with them.

Perhaps Melinda has fish at home. She knows what she wants to do and uses resources to help her achieve it. Pat is an unfamiliar adult but perhaps Melinda feels this about all the adults in the setting at this point; yet she trusts adults to have information that can help her. She is persistent and resourceful and seems a competent explorer of and gets back on the chair to watch the fish.

This observation lasts approximately 45 minutes.

About two weeks later, on film, we see Melinda outside with Zack and Tina, playing alongside them at 'dinosaurs'. She does not say much but runs around the area with them and is deeply engrossed in the play and very much a part of the trio. Zack and Tina are almost a year older than Melinda.

this new environment although she did not go outdoors during the morning.

Melinda may already be exploring possibilities for friendship and certainly sees a play theme ongoing that she can connect with.

Vignette 18: Amir watches

In contrast, Amir, also a new child, is relatively immobile in these early days of entry to the unit.

Amir watches

Amir is new, having attended for about two weeks at this point. His mother leaves him after entering the setting with him and speaking to the staff. Both Amir and his mother have English as a second language. He does not cry when his mother says goodbye but watches her till she disappears and then turns to look at the setting. She speaks to him in the family language as she leaves.

He moves a few steps forward and then stops in the middle of the room. A member of staff passes and says 'hello' to Amir, using his name. He looks but does not reply. Another asks him what he thinks he would like to do today. Amir does not reply and she tells him to 'have

Reflecting on Amir's observations

Amir's challenge is far greater than that of Melinda as he does not yet have much English to help him gain clues to how this new environment will operate. However, he seems able to think about engagement in the setting without too much distress being evident at this point.

Perhaps this movement signals a desire to engage but also a remaining uncertainty about with what or whom. Staff do discuss his 'slow settling' and are aware of his needs. Debbie comments: 'He just seems to need a lot of time to look around but a little think about it then'. He moves another step or two and watches some children in the home corner. He looks around. Other children and adults flow by him; one adult gives him a smile and 'thumbs up'; he smiles briefly. He looks at the door to the outdoor area but does not move towards it. He looks hesitant but unafraid. He occasionally looks across at adults working with groups or talking to playing children.

This episode lasts about 20 minutes and he then agrees to go with his key worker to an activity indoors.

someone usually takes him to play after a while.'

It does seem that he is not only watching but thinking also; perhaps building up internal images of how adults and children operate in this large indoor space. He seems aware of the outdoors but, as yet, not ready to engage with it.

Melinda is a confident and very active explorer. Amir seems not so physically confident but he seems alert to and interested in the wider activity and content to remain secure in this known space where his mother left him. As time goes on, adults do engage Amir in activities but they do not force him to move anywhere; he is taken only if it seems he wishes to go. New children were often seen standing in the doorway watching the outside play but choosing to remain indoors, presumably at that time a more familiar space for them. Moss and Petrie (2002) talk of 'children's spaces' as being a more relevant construct than that of 'children's services'. 'Children's spaces' refers not only to the physical environment in which they might find themselves coming together with adults and with other children but also to the different contexts in which they might find themselves engaging with adults and children within and across those environments (Dahlberg and Moss 2005). The concept of the meeting place carries with it, in these contexts, a strong notion of children's spaces as sites where 'meanings can be exchanged' (Clark 2010: 14). Perhaps, at this stage, when Melinda and Amir look towards the outdoor space they do not, as yet, see it as a space where they might make meaning because its meanings are not yet clear to them, so they take an interest but avoid engagement. Perhaps Amir still feels the same about the indoor space; he wants to build a better understanding of what adults and children do in this space before he begins to do it himself. Undergraduate students in their early days at university seem to have similar feelings in relation to the library; they express concerns which reveal they feel they may not act appropriately or that they may look in some way 'inexperienced', and so are self-conscious and reluctant to enter this initially daunting space.

During one of their discussions whilst watching film, Andy and Pat reflected further on this need for all the children to 'map' the space as a part of the progression towards play mastery. At this point in time, Andy and the team had recently undertaken reorganisation in the indoor area to create a space for the stage and a larger area for the large construction – both seen as important open-ended spaces for the indoor area, a concept that arose from the discussions and reflections by the team as discussed in Chapter 3. They had removed some netting that had been used to create a den (Figure 3.2) because they felt that the children were not using it. Like the stage, it had been introduced at an early point in redesigning the indoor space, but, as Andy suggests here, was subsequently removed and the space developed differently. Here, Andy and Pat reflect on how they are changing their understandings of what children see and do in new spaces as they repeatedly study the filmed materials:

Pat: But when a new area or new space is introduced, it almost feels as if there is a regression in the play in that place, in their understanding of it.

Andy: At the beginning they do a lot of watching.

Pat: Just moving things around as well, as if they're becoming familiar with them.

Andy: Sometimes there are quite short spells just right at the beginning of the day, as if they're looking around to see who's here and sorting it out in their heads before they get into it and then they get straight into it.

Pat: It does illustrate the fact that it's a new area, the materials are all familiar but they've moved to a different space and they're trying to get that sense of, they've got to try and understand again what it can do; build that picture again of what it can do.

Andy: Yes. We've also got a lot of children who do watch.

Pat: And it reminds me of when we talked about new children moving around the whole of the area and they've got to map it. It's as if these children have got to map this bigger space again and understand what it can do because things have changed in it.

Andy: I'm much more aware of how much they notice about the room. I've had loads of children who've come up to me this morning and said 'The netting's gone'.

Pat: When we looked at the film this morning, one of the children said 'Oh look, there's the netting' as if they were reminding themselves that it had been there but now it's gone.

Andy: Yes and it didn't seem to get used much; we took it down because they didn't seem to be using it much at all, it hadn't been used that much but they've all missed it.

Pat: So they'd mapped the area; they know when things change; they have to build new ways of thinking about the new resources, the new reference points.

Having explored this concept of 'mapping the early years space' and its importance for new children in building a meaningful understanding of their environment, and for established children in re-engaging with changed spaces, we want to move on to explore the development of four children, as they progress from new to experienced players in the unit. Charley, Patience, Sebastian and Rebecca have each been mentioned in previous vignettes throughout the book. Because of the longitudinal nature of the filming, we have all four children on film over the period of the research. We did not set out to 'capture' case studies; as was stated in Chapter 1, the filming was relatively random. There was no deliberation in terms of focussing on these four children but they appear sufficiently often, and over time, to allow some insights into their playful progression in this open-ended early years setting. These are not comprehensive pictures of each child's development but glimpses into their interests, engagements and activities as caught on film. The case studies do not offer an analysis of each child's progress; neither can it be claimed that there are significant similarities in their individual routes to mastery. However, once the case studies have been presented reflections are offered.

Four case studies of playful progression

Charley

Charley started at Fishergate as a young three-year-old. His brother, Stevie, an older four-year-old, was also in the early years unit at Fishergate alongside Charley. Stevie was a confident boy who had a well-established group of friends, all boys, and all of whom are seen many times on film, playing outside, making dens, ramps, bridges, often physically active and with a lot of conversation, discussion and argument as integral to their play. Charley had some difficulties settling in at first and his mother decided to keep him at home for a few weeks and to try a delayed start later in the term, after discussions with Andy. This seemed to suit Charley.

Towards the end of the summer term, a short time after restarting, we see Charley playing alone with the doll's house. He is deeply engrossed as he manipulates the figures and the furniture. He moves a figure up the stairs and briefly stops to watch the girls working on the boat design with Debbie (Chapter 4) but this is momentary. He stays about 15 minutes and then walks away. Pat's observational notes capture him a little time later, looking through the door to the outdoor area where Stevie is playing but Charley does not go out. He watches Stevie for a short time as he moves around the outdoor area in his play with his friends.

At the beginning of the autumn term, his brother's last term in the early years setting, Charley is outside playing with Stevie and his friends. The older boys are clustered around something in the corner and Charley goes to them and says: 'What you found?' He walks across to Pat and says: 'They've found woodlice under the shed.' Charley moves amongst them but does not seem as connected to them as they are connected to one another. He rolls his cars down a piece of guttering he has propped against a low wall. Stevie comes to watch. Charley goes to look when one boy finds a ladybird. He watches the boys discussing whether or not the peas that are growing here are dead, walking around the group and looking and listening but not joining in the discussions.

Later in the morning he is with Stevie and Marco in an area enclosed by a low wall. They have built a ramp up to the enclosing wall with a wide plank. Charley climbs the ramp to stand on the seat attached to the wall. He jumps from the wall into the area to reclaim his car. A ramp has been located leading into the enclosed area and Charley, Stevie and Marco are pushing their cars down the ramp to see which can go furthest; Marco is measuring distance with sticks. They do this several times, taking it in turns. Charley seems an equal participant in this play. He complains at one point, saying: 'Why don't I get to have the fastest car?' When he wins, he cheers and shouts: 'I won.' He cleans the wheels on his T-shirt when his car goes in a puddle. He smiles and laughs a lot and watches as Stevie and Marco change the design of the area. He does not contribute to the design activity.

About two weeks later we see Charley on the assault course that Roxanne initially designed (Chapter 2, vignette 3). He is playing away from other children. He walks carefully on the plastic water containers. One wobbles and he climbs carefully off it and goes to speak to Marco, who is helping to design the course. Charley then walks quickly and with confidence on a long line of low wooden bricks. He jumps and bounces along the crates and comes again to the wobbly water carrier. He gets down and turns the plastic container over and tries again but it is still wobbly so he goes around it and continues on the course, still alone. He is seen again a few minutes later when many more children are attracted to the assault course and he joins a long line of children patiently waiting for the course to be extended. Charley does not appear to speak to anyone else at this time but looks around and is smiling and seems relaxed.

We then see Charley just after Christmas, at the play dough where pipe cleaners are also available. He has made a hedgehog and is chatting to another boy (Stevie has now gone into Year 1). He chooses his pieces of pipe cleaner very carefully and seems very focussed. The other boy leaves as Charley is saying: 'My hedgehog is better than yours.' He remains here alone for some time and chats to Patience when she comes to get some of the pipe cleaners for a box she is filling. She is playing at magic potions.

In the final period of filming, Charley is one of the older five-year-olds in his final term and we see him with Aroon as they seek to melt the ice outdoors (Chapter 5, vignette 9). Charley keeps up a constant commentary on their activity and identifies many of the ideas for moving the activity forward. His language is peppered with: 'I've got a good idea'; 'I know, let's . . .' One idea for smashing the ice is to get long tubes and apply pressure to the ice in the bottle. At one point he says to Aroon 'You hold it while I smash it in'; he applies carefully aimed prods at the bottle of ice. When he finally succeeds in breaking out a large chunk of ice, he runs to Andy to show it to him. He brings it across to Pat to show her also, smiling: 'Look, I crashed it out.' Pat praises him, 'Well done.' He goes off to show other children and Aroon follows him. He gives a piece of ice to another boy. Later we see Charley and Aroon and they have put the ice in a bucket and are watching it melt. Charley fetches a cable reel to sit on and Aroon fetches a bread crate. They gather round the bucket, discussing what is happening to the ice. At one point they both laugh and Charley shouts at Pat 'It can talk' and they laugh again. He says: 'It looks pretty.' They both stand and carry the bucket carefully away across the outdoor area. Later, they are chatting to Andy and telling him what has happened to the ice; they still have it in the bucket. Later we see him running across the playground, still with the bucket and shouting: 'I've got an idea.' He gets a spade, calls out 'We've got some digging to do' and retrieves a piece of ice from under a tyre using the spade. Aroon uses the spade to prise the tyre from the floor and Charley reaches underneath for the ice. He runs to the outdoor tap calling: 'It needs washing.' Aroon follows him. Later we see Charley picking small pieces of ice from the floor and placing them in the bucket, saying 'Ice, ice, ice.' Aroon is fetching water to place in the bucket but only very small amounts. There are four boys involved in the activity now, all closely interacting with much conversation. The sense of shared goals is very strong across the group and Charley seems to lead much of the play with his ideas and suggestions.

Next day, he and five other boys are making their ice machine. Charley announces 'We'll have a great time' and they yell 'Yeah'. Charley also announces; 'We're making it for polar bears.' Aroon shouts 'Let's get water and make big ice' and some of the boys run off. Charley stays close to the 'machine' and looks at a new boy who has wandered over to see what they are doing. They bring water and throw it inside. At one point Elizabeth comes over and one boy announces to her: 'We are trying to make a big ginormous ice cube and Cole is trying to take it.' Elizabeth registers she has heard with a facial expression but makes no comment. Charley watches and listens to the children talking and looks inside the red tube where the water is being placed. Cole returns and one boy points and shouts: 'What about Cole?' Charley says quietly: 'Cole, you cannot take our ice, we need it. You can take some off the roof if you want.' Cole waits a while and, when the boys are in conversation, reaches inside, takes a large piece of ice and runs back to the pirate ship that others are building. Later we see Cole running off with another large piece of ice and Charley pursuing him across the area, calling his name. Cole runs over to stand beside a visiting mother and Charley tells her what is happening, saying: 'I had it first.' He walks away when the mother seems unable to resolve it in his favour but later we see Charley and Aroon with Cole, trying to wrestle the ice from him. The ice drops and breaks, Cole runs off with one piece and the two boys secure the other pieces, laughing. Charley comes to Pat and says: 'Cole nicked some ice but we let him have a bit.'

In the afternoon, Charley stays indoors. We see him engrossed in conversation with a girl, in a corner. Three of his friends 'hang around' but do not seem to be part of the play. Charley follows the girl across the indoor area to another corner and then they return to their first space, the other boys trailing after them. Charley and the girl are deep in conversation. Robbie brings a picture for Charley and says he has made it for him. Charley goes to put it in his drawer and returns to his corner. Robbie stays and seems to want to draw Charley's attention to him but Charley does not seem interested in talking to Robbie although he does not actively reject him. Later we see that Charley has joined Rebecca and the girls in the stage area and seems to be an integral part of their play; there is a lot of eye contact, smiles, conversation and laughter as their play progresses to a 'wedding' scenario. Aroon is present but his involvement seems more peripheral.

Rebecca

The first time we see Rebecca on camera, she is a new three-year-old, outside in her wellingtons, playing alone and stamping in a puddle. She jumps across the puddle. She walks around the puddle. Owen, four years old, speaks to her; she listens but does not follow him. As he moves away she continues jumping, with one foot or two feet, and kicking the water. Later, Owen has returned and watches her jumping and splashing and then walks away again. He goes to stand in another puddle and then Rebecca goes over to him. There is at least a year's difference in their ages, but Owen does not have close friends at this time and often plays alone. They play together, throwing and fetching a ball and walking around. At one point Owen picks up a plastic crate and carries it around for a long time. Rebecca climbs on and jumps off reels and Owen copies her, Rebecca climbs on a wall. She gets a small spade and carries water from the puddle to a plastic container and drops it onto the container. She does this several times and then attempts to fill the container with the water. Owen watches her, still carrying the plastic crate.

Rebecca is seen again, later in the day, with Owen again, in the powder paint activity with Andy and Debbie (Chapter 5, vignette 14). She says very little but is deeply engrossed, occasionally laughing and clapping her hands and fetching and spreading powder paint; she stays for around 20 minutes.

The next time we see her is three weeks later, on a warm day, and she is walking alone around the outdoor area. She looks at Kat, the student teacher, standing on a large tyre, smiles at her, climbs up on the tyre beside her and begins to circle her, walking sideways with small steps. Later we see her filling a large bucket at the outdoor tap and walking across the outdoor area, clearly knowing where she is going; a little later we see her emerging from the indoor area still carrying her bucket and walking purposefully. A little later, she is walking indoors chatting to another girl. Later we see her playing in the sand with the same girl.

Two weeks later, we see Rebecca in the outdoor area with two of the five-year-olds; one of them hugs her and the other holds her hand. One says to her 'You are a little one' but Rebecca replies 'I'm bigger now.' Rebecca and the girl holding her hand walk indoors together. These are the girls who are making the boat with Debbie; they had commented (Chapter 4) on 'fetching Rebecca to go in the boat with them'.

A week later, she approaches two boys who are digging in a small, circular central garden area, where a small tree is growing. She watches them as they dig with their hands. They seem to be ignoring her. She approaches Pat and says she wants to play with them so Pat asks the boys: 'Boys, can Rebecca play with you, she says she wants to play with you?' One boy replies: 'Well, we're playing dirty making things.' Pat asks again: 'Is that all right, if she plays?' The other boy holds up his hands and says: 'Yeah but you need to get dirty.' Rebecca touches the soil and he repeats: 'But I mean, really, really dirty.' The other boy responds 'Yeah, look how dirty we are' and the two boys hold their hands up for Rebecca to see them. Rebecca does not reply but transfers some soil from one part of the garden to another on a small spade. One boy lifts some greenery up and says 'Plant hair.' Rebecca looks. His friend puts some greenery on a pine cone, lifts it up and says 'Look, I'm a lady with plant hair'; all three laugh. The play continues but the boys interact only with each other. Rebecca looks at them occasionally; she seems to like walking around the circular garden and changing the location of her play space. The boys throw pine cones at the tree, shouting 'Shoot it off' repeatedly. Rebecca watches with apparent interest but does not copy them.

About 15 minutes later we see her holding hands with Melinda, who is around the same age as Rebecca. They enter the design that Archie and Luke have built (Chapter 2, vignette 2) by the 'door'. Rebecca stands beside Melinda and watches what Archie is doing. Archie offers an explanation to Melinda and Rebecca about what everything is in the house. Rebecca listens with attention and interest. Rebecca and Melinda then leave, down the corridor and out through the 'door', still holding hands. Rebecca goes over to watch Patience, who is with Paul and another boy, sitting on cable reels.

Several months later, in the final period of filming, we find Rebecca at the writing table at the start of the day along with three other girls of her age-group. She has finished a drawing and is carefully folding her paper. She speaks to the girl next to her 'My cat has very sharp claws'; a conversation ensues between the two girls for several minutes. Rebecca unfolds her picture and uses glue to secure the folds. She says half to herself 'I'll put it in my drawer. It's a bit rubbish but, oh well', and goes off. She returns and takes an interest in what a new, visiting child is doing, speaking briefly to her. A few days later, first thing in the morning, Rebecca is at the table again, with one boy and a girl. She is drawing and cutting. Another girl comes and kneels on the floor beside her and they begin a conversation for several minutes as Rebecca draws, writes, cuts and sticks.

A little later we see Rebecca outside. She goes to see what Charley is doing (the ice machine) and he explains what they are making. She looks and listens for a while and a little later we see her with another girl chalking on the outside board. They stay there for about 25 minutes and then we see Rebecca in the outdoor sand pit, playing alongside Sebastian and Cole. She and Sebastian are in conversation.

In the afternoon, Rebecca climbs up the steps and onto the stage area, where three other girls are playing. One girl has her arm around Rebecca's shoulders and seems to be trying to facilitate her entry to the play as she chats to the two other girls. It seems to be agreed and quite a long four-way conversation ensues. Two boys arrive to pursue a 'monsters' scenario; Rebecca engages with them but seems more 'patient' than 'enthralled', as if she finds their play a little bit 'silly'. The boys move away, perhaps sensing a lack of interest. Over the next half hour the group of four girls move a wide range of resources from elsewhere in the room into the stage area and seem to be following a domestic play scenario; it is not possible to hear them. Just after the point when Charley joins them, Rebecca takes a cloth and begins spreading it on the floor inside the stage area; she and Charley hug one another, smile and chat. Later, she is spreading the cloth again and Charley is helping her; they are smiling and chatting and Aroon is chatting with them. It is a wedding theme. Charley and Rebecca go down the steps; Charley dances with Rebecca saying: 'Men and ladies do that, and mums and dads.' Rebecca smiles at him; they process around the indoor area and return to the stage. Play continues for some time with much interaction, smiling and joint action; Rebecca spreads a larger cloth outside the stage area and another girl is helping her. They are smiling and chatting and talking about 'making food for the wedding'. Later Rebecca and her friend spread the cloth on the floor just beyond the stage area 'for the wedding food, because lots of people are coming'.

Sebastian

When Sebastian began, his large and small motor skills were not well developed although his interest in exploring his environment was strong. He is often seen alone on film, striding very purposefully in the outdoor area, often wearing a hat. Sebastian has English as a second language and had very little English when he first attended the early years unit.

Sebastian has already been described at some length in Chapter 3, vignette 4, where he and Ashley, both quite new in the unit, played extensively with the red tube and with bricks. We also saw him briefly, and in conflict with Archie and Luke, in Chapter 2, vignette 2, when the two boys sought to prevent him from entering their outdoor design. You might recall that Sebastian threw a small plank in anger at them at that time because he was refused entry.

Towards the end of the summer term, about four weeks later, we see Sebastian outside playing alone with cars on a cable reel; about 20 minutes later he is standing beside the computers watching a boy play but not playing himself. He brings a large wooden brick to where the girls are designing the boat with Debbie, kneels down and places it on their paper, and then walks away. One of the girls doing the design removes it when she returns with her tube for the paddle she is making. Sebastian does not seem to return to this activity.

A week or so later, we see Sebastian alongside the children on the assault course, just as their play is drawing to a close. He is wearing his pirate hat, in which he has been coming to school for several weeks now. He walks unsteadily on some crates away from the queuing children, in the opposite direction but still on the assault course. He turns back and waves and smiles at someone and then walks back towards the 'queue'. He walks on an upturned milk crate and wobbles quite strongly but carries on and then falls from the next crate to the floor. He looks a little upset but does not cry and walks beside the course, rubbing his side. He goes inside with the other children as it is time for lunch. His face is angry and he is muttering to himself as he deals with his injury.

A week or so later we see him engaged in the play with the red tube with Ashley (Chapter 3, vignette 4). After this play, he tries to take a watering can from Patience; she successfully protects the object, as we have also seen in the same vignette. Sebastian moves on from this to an extended and absorbed engagement with the water tray and with pouring water down a grate, an activity that Debbie says he was engaged in, with great concentration, the day before. He turns a large plastic car on its side and fills it with water, simulating putting in petrol as he puts water where the petrol cap is. What Sebastian does not seem to realise is that another boy was playing in the car, had gotten out briefly and was upset when he returned to find he could not return to his car. Sebastian continues filling it with 'petrol'. When the boy tries to return the car to an upright position Sebastian pushes him away, looking at him angrily. The boy moves away and continues to watch Sebastian; he looks upset but does not seek an adult. Sebastian continues to fill it with 'petrol' for some time before returning to the water tray and running water down the ramps and watching it for several minutes. The other boy reclaims his car.

In the final period of filming, Sebastian, in the term before he goes into Year 1, is dressed as Spider-Man and playing with three other boys in the enclosed area, which has now become an outdoor sand pit; Sebastian's father, who is a builder, helped to make the sandpit. The boys are digging and pouring water into the holes. Although it is icy cold outside, Sebastian sits down and takes his shoes and socks off and returns to the sand. He offers commentaries on his actions and his English is well developed. He removes his Spider-Man hat: 'I'm going to take this off. I don't want it any more'. He gives it to a boy on the wall and returns to his digging. He pulls his trousers up above his knees and kneels in the sand. He moves around the area purposefully, singing at one point 'La, la, la, la, la, la, la la, la, la, la, la, laaa, laaa' and then repeating this as he digs. His song is very tuneful. He carries sand carefully from one hole to another and repeats his song. He smoothes the sand carefully, taking his time and using small, well-controlled movements. He stands and walks around the sand pit, watching the sand as he grinds it beneath his bare toes. He seems to be enjoying the tactile sensation of the sand beneath his feet.

About 20 minutes later, we see Sebastian with two other boys and a large plastic container with water in it. They are each holding one handle and running across the outdoor area. Sebastian is laughing. They are coming from the water tap and, having crossed the area, empty the container into a hollowed-out tree trunk. One boy calls 'One more time' and Sebastian replies 'Oh yeah.' He gets hold of the container with the two boys and they run back to the tap. A few minutes later we see him being chased around the outdoor area by another boy with a stick. Both are laughing and Sebastian is shouting: 'Chasing, chasing, chasing.'

A few minutes later, he has the Spider-Man hat back on and is climbing onto a construction that some other boys are making. They are making 'the Olympic stadium' with cable reels and other materials; this building had been much in the news at that time. Sebastian watches as they bring more materials to add to what is there. He walks around the design and tries to pull out a piece of tubing which is trapped. He succeeds and moves away with it.

Next day, Sebastian is watching Aroon, who has piled up three cable reels on a tyre. Sebastian gently touches another boy who is talking and smiles at him. He jumps from the tyre, announces 'I will get some water' and runs towards the tap. He returns to the construction with a long pole which he sweeps to and fro like a sword. He climbs onto the cable reels and to the top of the structure carrying his 'sword'. He sits and watches the others who are designing around him; the design gradually becomes a pirate ship. He climbs down at one point saying 'This will be the best pirate ship ever'; later we see him back in the centre with his 'sword'. He announces 'Get the sword, we need to get the sword', and he and another boy run off. One boy chases Sebastian around the area; he and two other boys play fight with the swords and then return to the 'ship'. At one point, we see Sebastian looking at a map that Robbie has made and they are discussing it.

Patience

Early observations of Patience's entry to Fishergate show several occasions when there were tears. One day, she left something behind when the children went to the hall and cried until she was taken to find it. She seemed deeply upset by this and took several minutes to recover once back in the unit. Also, during this period, she is captured on film, walking in the outdoor area, alone, but with her jug as she moves water from one place to another.

Some weeks later we see Patience taking an interest in the play of Ashley and Sebastian around the big red tube (Chapter 3, vignette 4). They are dropping bricks into it. She watches them for a few minutes and then skips off to walk on a low wall. She returns as Ashley shouts 'There's a spider in it'; Patience looks into the tube again with great interest and then at Ashley. She skips off again, goes again to climb on the central low wall and walks on it. She speaks to no one although her language is well developed.

A little later in the morning, we see her in the enclosed area outdoors. She collects something in a container and skips across the outdoor area with it, holding it high. She chats to a boy who returns with her to the enclosed area. We see them together, and then we see Patience is looking again into the red tube; she still has a container in her hand, and briefly has an open umbrella which she drops on the floor. Someone else picks it up and we see her then with another umbrella. She still has the umbrella when she returns to Ashley and Sebastian using the red tube. There is an altercation ongoing and Patience stands close to Sebastian who has a raised brick. She holds her hand close to him and in front of her own face and he lowers the brick. She watches with great concentration as the student teacher, Kat, comes to speak to the two boys.

Later the same morning, we see her taking a plastic bottle to the outdoor tap and filling it and returning to where a small group are gathered. She pours the water into something as the others watch her; this is her fire scenario with Paul, mentioned in Chapter 3. Then we see her passing Sebastian with a watering can and a spade. Sebastian tries to take the watering can from her. She does not call out or look upset but she resists him firmly by holding tightly to the watering can. The student teacher intervenes and Sebastian lets go. Patience offers him the spade but he throws it on the floor. Patience returns to the tap with her watering can to refill the now empty container. Sebastian follows and watches over her shoulder but she turns away from him and shields the watering can from his view. He stamps away and Patience takes her water to the same small group to fill the inside of a set of plastic steps where Paul is still putting out fires. She skips off to fill it again; Sebastian sees her and goes to take the watering can. Patience resists him, not speaking or calling out but hanging firmly on to the green watering can with a determined look on her face. She resists him success-fully and Pat takes Sebastian indoors to look for another container.

About two months later we see Patience emerging from a den outdoors and chasing Paul around the outdoor area while carrying a rope and laughing. Later the same morning, we see her at the hammering bench. She watches the chil-dren there and then goes to search for a piece of wood. A short time later she returns outside to where Archie and Luke have been building their telescope but are now building the ramp for water (Chapter 4, vignette 8). She goes to the water tap, fills a container and takes the water over to Kat to let it flow down the ramp. She walks over to watch Archie as he guides the ramp (made from gutter-ing) into the shallow tray that Andy has brought to collect the water, which was running over the floor. Patience runs her hand up and down the ramp, looks at the tray again and skips away across the playground. She returns quickly with a crate, places it beside the ramp where she was recently standing and sits on it. She runs her hand up and down the guttering ramp several times as the water is coming down. She goes inside, returns again without her baseball cap and sits down. She watches with interest when Debbie places an obstacle on the ramp to see if the water will 'go around it or push it down' and shouts: 'push it down'. She is correct and smiles. She gets the 'obstacle' (a piece of Blu-Tack), repeats the experiment and then pushes it down into the shallow tray. She repeats it again and laughs when it goes on the floor. She retrieves it and tries again.

We then see her towards the end of the summer term in the outdoor area with Paul in almost the same part of the outdoor area as when they were previously playing at fires. Patience is bringing plastic containers to their den and they disappear inside it for much of the time. We see her following Paul across the outdoor area and 'firing' her short tube at other children as she passes. She climbs on a cable reel and Paul and another boy join her. A little later she is seen walking around near the enclosed area where the two boys she was with earlier are still playing. About 20 minutes later, the three of them are still playing together around the cable reel and Patience is seen carrying water over very carefully; the two boys are seated and pushing something into the bottles they have. Patience goes again for water, carrying it carefully in a shallow tray.

The observational notes record Patience making potions on several occasions, throughout the filming period; she returns to this activity many times, over several months. She uses the indoors and the outdoors with confidence, often walking purposefully around, collecting materials and placing them in different containers. Some inner plan seems to be guiding her actions; her behaviour appears to be goal-orientated.

The next time we see Patience on film, is during the autumn term, indoors, her final term before going into Year 1. She is at a table with lots of natural autumn materials on it: pine cones, pine branches, leaves, twigs and so on. She is collecting the materials into a small plastic box, breaking some twigs to get them in. We see her walking around with her box in her hand and then she returns to the table to put more materials into it. As she does so she is chatting to a girl who also has a collection of natural materials in a plastic bottle. Later, we see Patience with Charley at the play dough table and she is collecting pipe cleaners to place in her plastic box. She does not speak to Charley although he describes what he is doing to Patience and does not seem worried that she does not answer.

When Pat returned for the final period of filming, Patience was in Year 1. However, one day whilst Pat was standing near the fence filming, Patience came over to her and said: 'I remember you.' The conversation continued:

> *Pat:* From when you were in the early years unit?
> *Patience:* Yes, I'm in Year 1 now.
> *Pat:* I remember you. You used to like to play at magic potions.

Patience looks thoughtful, then nods and smiles.

> *Pat:* Do you still play at that?
> *Patience:* No, not much. Well, a bit. Last week when it was cold, I made some in the ice. Then it melted. But not much.
> *Pat:* Do you play at other things now?
> *Patience:* [nods and then] But I still play with Paul at superheroes.

Patience skips off.

Reflecting on the case studies

The case studies give insights into the ways in which these four children visit and revisit their interests on a day-to-day basis and how this might help to deepen their individual understanding and knowledge of the issues that flow from their interests and preoccupations. Each of them, at their own pace and in their own way, develops their capacities for interacting with other children whilst pursuing these interests, and for finding and regularly engaging with children who have similar interests. Their interests do not only manifest themselves through language, although, when it is possible to hear and listen to their conversations, these do reveal the extent of the knowledge already in place and in particular the use of humour as they become older. We also get a strong sense of them as reflective thinkers and as perpetually goal-orientated and can see how the organisational structure of the unit and its associated routines give them extended periods of time for thinking and watching and for planning and achieving their personally initiated goals.

The case studies also show the extent to which their learning is rooted in movement, wandering, running, skipping, stomping, jumping, chasing, walking, following, leading, building, play fighting, crawling, climbing, falling and so on. In their self-selected learning modes, movement prevails; the movement seems to tie the ideas together or perhaps it helps to liberate the ideas, or perhaps both. Their learning does not occur at one activity or on one day, over a week or over a month; it appears that the days and weeks of linked activities that emerge from their personal interests and prior experiences become shared with like-minded peers, and movement is also an important part of that sharing. Their 'learning outcomes' are internalised processes that are often manifest only through language, action and interaction. The play is both the catalyst for and the expression of their learning. As these four children have built their confidence and learned to map the environment and the materials in it, they have become better able to combine and use those materials in more complex ways, to match the developing complexity of their interactive play themes.

What does become evident across these case studies is the extent to which each of the children, as they become older, engages in high levels of problem-solving, language-based activities, and the extent to which cooperative activities prevail, with quite large groups of children coming together to create and sustain extended scenarios that chime with their own lives and experiences. Yet each of them has started from solitary activity in the unit, and two of them from being especially unsettled when they started in the unit. In this environment they have:

- the space to be solitary;
- the chance to interact with others in passing;
- the space to make and then be with friends;
- the space to argue and disagree;

- the space to be affectionate and share humour;
- the space to separate and to return together;
- the space to run and imagine;
- the space to be assertive;
- the space to think and observe;
- the space to become a leader in aspects of their play.

Once they have learned to map these indoor and outdoor spaces, they learn to manage the spaces and themselves within them in creative and exploratory ways. As time goes by, the spaces have greater meaning for them because they have inhabited these spaces, with their own thoughts and ideas, on a regular basis. Their memories of themselves as players and meaning-makers in these spaces are rich and vibrant and seem to continue to inform their playful learning far beyond what any adult might be capable of directly planning for them. These areas, both indoors and outdoors, carry 'imprints' of their own past actions and interactions in similar ways to those Clark (2010) describes in her work on the transformations of children's spaces. What adult would suggest:

- making 'an ice machine . . . for the polar bears' (Charley) or
- asking Archie and Luke to explain the purposes of their design in detail (as Rebecca received from Archie's spontaneous expressions) or
- taking your shoes and socks off on an icy day (Sebastian) or
- developing a year-long interest in magic potions (Patience)?

We would argue that only child-initiated activities could create these and many other 'whatever you want them to be' spaces and places.

The children are shown as each being able to express their own identity and explore their own personality, and to gain a better sense of self. By observing their play, the early years team also get to know the children well in this open-ended environment and they get a chance to think about ways of extending that environment to match the children's expressed play themes and interests. Each child's personality and identity is evident as the children ebb and flow together in their play. There is vitality evident in their actions and choices, whether solitary or cooperative, and a strong sense of both spontaneity and deep engagement is juxtaposed in their play.

The final chapter draws together some insights and reflections drawn from this longitudinal study of open-ended play spaces and the 'whatever you want it to be place' in one early years unit.

Chapter 7

Understanding the power, the possibilities and the challenges of the 'whatever you want it to be place' within the early years

Chapter 1 talked about 'the complexity of play', as indeed do many publications on play. It explored the notion that one of the reasons why it is challenging for high status to be given to play is because those complexities are difficult to convey in a simple way. Play looks simple; expert players make it looks easy and that is in part because, in the right kind of environment, the learning is masked by the pleasure and engagement of those play experiences that are initiated by children to chime with their own themes, interests, experiences and cultural familiarities. By the same token, play is a social activity for much of the time, subject to the influence of many variables; because of this, play narratives and engagements are difficult to 'capture' through research. We hope that these rich, qualitative vignettes, with child and adult commentaries and interpretation, are helpful in supporting these concluding comments.

By that same token, the book has made no claims that providing the 'right kind of environment' is easy. Andy puts it well in the following reflection in a conversation undertaken with Pat after the filming had finished:

> This is challenging and I think that working in this way – when I talk to other teachers they sometimes seem to think it's very simple and a straight-forward way of working. They think that by working like this we are doing less. But we're not; I think we're doing far more. We're spending less time doing some of the more structured things, the more formal teaching, although we still do them, but more time observing the play, interacting with the play and using the play as the basis of our planning and then going forward with it. To work like this, I think you have to develop skills. It's not a simple way to work at all. It's something that you get right sometimes and wrong sometimes. It's not something you can just plan and get right all of the time. It's complex to understand what is happening as they play, then trying to add something into it; that is, if you do need to add something . . . I think we get better over time at making those judgements about when to stand back and watch.

The preceding chapters have tried to unpick and make more explicit and achievable some of those complexities, both in the play itself and the ways in which provision for such play might be made by early years educators who want to try some of these approaches for themselves and for the children for whom they make provision. It's also worth bearing in mind that, although the early years team at Fishergate have created open-ended spaces indoors and outdoors, they started with a 'small' idea – how to bring more opportunities for open-ended play into the children's play experiences – and grew it from there because of what they saw the children doing and how they saw the children responding as they turned open-ended play spaces and materials into the their own 'whatever you want it to be place'.

Pat made an entry in her research journal towards the end of the research period:

> In my years observing children's play, I have never been so thoroughly and consistently surprised by what children are capable of in the right kind of learning environment as I have been when watching these children play and learn over these months of research at Fishergate.

The book has sought to describe and explore 'playful learning' and 'playful pedagogies' as ways of thinking about what children and adults might do, together and independently of one another in an early years setting, or unit in this case. It was beneficial to undertake the joint research in an early years unit because this brought older and very capable four- and five-year-olds into the orbit of data collection alongside the new and exploratory three- and younger four-year-olds. The chapters have explored how, in this early years unit, these children progressed from sometimes tentative and uncertain explorers of their environment to masterful, expert players capable of self-direction and cooperative engagement, designers of complex structures, problem-setters and solvers, risk-takers and adventurers, resilient individuals and happy and absorbed pupils. We have also made a case (we hope) for the positive impact of an open-ended play environment, in the hands of reflective, observant practitioners, in enabling children to achieve these states of being and so to enjoy being learners in school. Enjoyment is part of entitlement as children soak up the knowledge in the world around them through their self-initiated actions and interactions. We would maintain that, and intend to illustrate how, these children are soaking up knowledge on a daily basis.

This final chapter draws together, in three sections, what we have learned in undertaking this joint research. The first focusses on playful learning in the 'whatever you want it to be place'. The second considers the pedagogical creation of open-ended play opportunities in an early years setting. The third returns to discussions around balance between child-initiated and teacher-initiated activities in an early years setting and considers future possibilities with a revised Early Years Foundation Stage awaiting confirmation as the book goes into production.

Playful learning in the 'whatever you want it to be place'

This space has been described in the model that has been explored throughout the book as: *the environment and its possibilities as perceived and engaged with from the child's perspective*. Children enter a space where anything is possible – whether a large or small space – and where they can engage alone or with others in exploring and exploiting that environment to match the images, plans and memories that emerge from their own minds, experiences and skills.

The book has drawn initially from Vygotskyan perspectives which value and examine play within the mental and intellectual development of children (Vygotsky 1966), and from socio-cultural theoretical perspectives on play, exploring the child's play in communities of players and communities of learners (Rogoff 1990, 2003). As Pramling-Samuelsson and Fleer (2009: 14) state: 'considering play as the leading activity in the development of young children is different to thinking about play as the "child's world" or the "child's work"'. These latter two terms are inexplicit and imply that no further understanding is required of playful engagements; but we would argue that deep understanding is needed. To call it their 'world' undermines its complexities and to call it their 'work' denies the sense of choice that can enter playful learning in the right circumstances.

Recent debates have emphasised the extent to which individual children bring their cultural heritages, languages and identities into their early years settings as primary reference points (Brooker 2002, 2010) and wider socio-cultural theory has sought to develop these theoretical reference points in recent years. We hope this book can make a contribution in this respect.

We have questioned the construct of 'uniqueness' for young children, not because we do not value it but because it is so all-encompassing that it has little meaning in relation to understanding playful learning and in subsequently determining playful pedagogies; in this way, it sits in the same category as the inexplicitness of 'child's work' and 'child's world'. The construct of 'uniqueness' cannot reveal the extent to which children have much in common in designing and executing their daily play themes in an open-ended play environment. The 18 vignettes and their interpretations have aimed to illustrate the extent to which, when children enter 'whatever you want them to be' places and spaces, their play themes and interests are revealed both as culturally personal and as having the potential to engender cooperative engagements with inherent intellectual challenges, as cultures and experiences coincide and mesh through playful engagements. Their individual play themes are unique because they draw from explorations and engagements with their own life experiences thus far and with their current memories of those experiences; but other children share those engagements with the world and, as the vignettes have shown, children's interests in how the world works and in how individuals interact in that world have a great deal in common. This notion of uniqueness might seem to bring profound additional complexities to an understanding of play if we think of 45 individuals expressing 'uniqueness' in play. However, the play themes are revealed as inter-connected across some groups of children and, as a consequence, can guide their choice of friends and regular playmates if they are allowed to engage regularly with both the themes and the friends.

After early periods of site exploration, beginning indoors where their confidence is greater, some children become interested in creating enclosures that explore aspects of their home lives, often doing this through animal play as well as family play. Immediately they bring their own home culture into the setting by replicating the patterns of home as best they can remember, depending on their age. We see younger children lying on shelves that have been emptied of bricks, covering themselves with fabric or just watching. We see older children creating larger, designed spaces and then 'furnishing' them. These might be shared experiences from home, as we saw in Archie and Luke's play in Chapter 2, cooperative play in the pursuit of their own domestic spaces, and vignette 5 in Chapter 3, where children were designing and inhabiting kennels in neighbourhoods. As Cosaro (1997) states, these kinds of playful activities reveal the extent to which children are capable of creating and participating in peer cultures through the day-to-day explorations of common experiences and understandings. We take that argument further and say that the open-endedness of the materials actively facilitates these identifications of common interests.

We see interests in exploring the work roles of parents, unique, perhaps in each individual child's perspective but a fundamental part of the human experience. Roxanna in vignette 3, we think, was building an assault course influenced by her mother's role in the army. Sebastian in vignette 4 seemed to be replicating his father's work as a builder with the use of the red tube as a cement mixer, whilst alongside him Ashley used the same resource to sustain play themes around fires and spiders. Play with fire was a play theme seen commonly across children, as something dangerous and in need of being managed enters their lives and consciousness. Magic potions was a perennial play theme with many younger children engaged with it on a regular basis, but even in Year 1 Patience still acknowledged it as a continuing, if diminishing, part of her life (Chapter 6).

The quest for physical challenge within the daily play environment is important for some children, both boys and girls. Roxanna may have been inspired to design the assault course because of her mother's work but many others, of all ages and both boys and girls, were inspired to use the environment to challenge themselves individually but within a collective enterprise. This vignette (Chapter 2) showed communities of learners at work but so did many other vignettes; several of these included risk-taking and overcoming physical fears, as shown in vignette 10 when the boys were building bridges and slides, and vignette 11 when children were swinging on pulleys. Remember how after the three older children had moved away Robbie copied the play but only to his own level of comfort. Here, at his own level and in his own time, he is learning to identify and meet the challenge of his own developing physical competences; and so begins his engagement with resilience and persistence as necessary characteristics in life. Arnold (2003) explores the extent to which physical movement is an integral part of her grandson's development over an extended period of time and illustrates in detail how this connects with his extended interest in particular play themes (as has also been illustrated at Fishergate) and the connections between physicality and learning for Harry. Robbie, a solitary player at this stage of his life, is seen later in the film as a part of Charley's highly interactive and cooperative play circle.

Generally speaking, educators seldom encourage younger children to watch and copy older children, but much of what we observed in the 'whatever you want it to be place' involved younger learners taking a deep interest in the designing of the older children. There were occasions at Fishergate where early years team members also sat and watched the play with groups of gathering children, but usually only when the children themselves had taken an interest in watching. In vignette 8 (Chapter 4), when Archie and Luke had built the telescope and then the structure for transferring water, younger children pulled up chairs and crates to watch them. In vignette 13 (Chapter 5), when Zack and friends made the 'rainbow river', as well as Robbie taking an interest here, others were captured on film stopping and watching in passing. Such action was captured many times. It is recognised as common in older children's playground play (Factor 2009) but perhaps can be more substantially incorporated into early years pedagogies also as a natural and important part of what children choose to do when activities of interest are going on around them. It seemed that the younger children were more intent on watching that which was unfamiliar, and probably beyond their zone of proximity and competence, than they were on watching activities that paralleled their own capacities for achievement.

These spaces have become shared sites of enterprise, places where children 'find themselves' as independent and autonomous individuals capable of collective endeavour, as they become older. In addition, the children design and inhabit spaces and play ideas that no adult would have thought of because the adult does not live the life of each child. In playing together they learn over time which other children have interests that parallel and reflect their own, and from these mutual engagements come levels of play complexity and depth that could only come from momentum-building and familiarity with peers and with the environment. Some children found this difficult at the outset. Sebastian as a second language learner comes to mind, but over time, in his own choice of 'whatever you want them to be' places, he made friends and gradually achieved joint enterprise with his own play ideas to the fore on occasion and a capacity for leadership beginning to emerge. The children's ideas and the possibilities associated with them mature and flourish in the children's own hearts, minds and brains.

In these ways then, and through their daily and extended engagement with 'whatever you want them to be' places and spaces, the early years setting becomes a space and place where children explore their identity, potential and interests and push back the boundaries of personal possibility through playful engagement by identifying and pursuing their own play themes alongside co-players, some of whom become friends. In the company of like-minded peers, they express their personalities, pursue their personal interests, form their identity and enhance their working knowledge of the world around them as increasingly powerful individuals who can shape and change their immediate environment through personal control, collective decision-making and expressions of, and on occasion negotiation of, personal choices.

Conflict and its resolution is a key part of children's lives and throughout the research we saw low-key but nonetheless important experiences of conflict and its resolution in evidence in the indoor and outdoor spaces. Only one example drew an adult (vignette 15), when Joe fetched Andy over to resolve issues with Cole. However, we also saw Joe exercising other assertive strategies with Cole in vignettes 14 and 15, the girls and their lizards did so in vignette 6, Sebastian was managed and still able to express himself in vignette 2, Ashley and Sebastian remained interactive in vignette 4 despite some initial jostling for position and access to the red tube, and we saw Charley and Patience in their extended profiles of Chapter 6 also asserting themselves with other children who sought to 'access' their resources. There were many examples of assertiveness from both boys and girls with some of them containing elements of conflict. However, in the majority of cases, the conflict was resolved by the children, without drawing adult intervention and invariably in quite low-key ways.

As stated at the beginning, we did not capture the children's voices within the study to the extent to which we had originally hoped and this was largely a logistical issue – finding the time and place to do it. There are certainly digital technologies now available that might make this much easier were the study to be repeated or replicated. However, we do believe that what we captured was powerful in revealing the capacities children have for understanding and expressing significance and meaning within their own play experiences. They certainly gave Andy and Pat insights into the play that they had not had the ability to recognise themselves from their own reflections on play action.

In order to develop as playful pedagogues, early years educators may need to be prepared to make a continuing study of playful learning in an environment where children's choices are encouraged, sustained and celebrated. This is perhaps part of what Andy means when he says: 'It's not a simple way to work at all.' The next section offers some concluding thoughts on implementing and sustaining playful pedagogies through open-ended play provision.

Playful pedagogies: creating open-ended play opportunities in an early years setting

The model that the book has explored has defined an open-ended play environment as follows: a way for the adult to conceive of her/his own role in creating and sustaining an educational environment that is flexible enough to allow children's interests and experiences to emerge and develop; it also encompasses the adults' responsibilities in identifying, recording and planning for those interests in systematic but flexible ways and a responsibility to look for ways of extending those interests and relating them to the wider world in which the child is living and learning.

At the end of the introduction it was stated that early years educators would need to decide for themselves the scale upon which they would undertake to make, sustain and develop open-ended play provision in their settings. Andy had started small in a previous school, with boxes and fabrics and structures to support den-making on an indoor carpet area. He had been impressed with and surprised by the quality, cooperation and absorption in children's play, as a wide range of play themes had built around the enclosures and structures that children had designed, often as cooperating groups. He had not seen such play before in his classroom. Play leaders had emerged who had ideas that could take their own and other children's play forward. He had taken these ideas to Fishergate with him and, over time, they had re-emerged to begin to influence thinking and practice across a wider team of early years educators. The extensive outdoor provision at Fishergate had developed from discussions across the early years team as some of these ideas had been reintroduced, with extensive support from parents as they brought in unanticipated amounts of and types of open-ended play materials. We heard in Chapter 5 from some visiting parents how they too had been initially surprised by the open-ended and rather unconventional nature of the provision, but had simultaneously come to see how much their own child and others enjoyed and engaged with the environment. Perhaps they began to see a capacity for exploration and risk-taking within their own children that they had not previously seen.

All the while, the early years team were working to and planning from the Early Years Foundation Stage curriculum requirements and were, additionally, developing the children's literacy and numeracy skills through small group, adult-led activities with the reception-aged children. However, their starting point for their practice was one of 'open-ended play' experiences for the children which allowed continuing and deep expression of play interests. Through their work and reflections together, the team explored the applications of these starting points to their outdoor and indoor play provision and to their planning, assessing and recording practices. Through their reflections and discussions they began to address the question of how educators can take the social and cultural experiences of the child into account when creating and sustaining a playful learning environment for large groups of children.

It was important to note, as we did in vignettes 7 and 8 (Chapter 4), the building of the boat with Debbie in Chapter 4 and vignette 14 (Chapter 5), that the adults here did initiate and engage with children in playful ways; however, on every observed/filmed occasion, the engagement was developed around the children's expressed or observed interests. In vignette 14, Andy initiated the powder paint play with Rebecca and Owen because he had observed them playing together the previous day, a significant step for both of them. Although

Owen was an older child and Rebecca a new child, they each tended to solitary play at this point in time and Andy had seen this as an opportunity to create peer engagement through a facilitative adult. They had been bouncing in puddles together the previous day (described in Rebecca's case study in Chapter 6) and so the idea of moving powder paint around with their feet on a large sheet of paper was an approximate replication, through adult direction, of the previously observed child-initiated activities. The engagement with the ice in a bottle (vignette 9, Chapter 5) had arisen from work around ice and freezing that Malcolm, the student teacher, had introduced, but this had been done during a period of intense cold weather; Chapter 2 listed 'weather' as an integral natural resource for supporting learning as, over time, the team had noted how weather influenced children's activities and the associated learning opportunities on a regular basis as the year in school progressed.

Although the early years team never discussed an intention to create a non-stereotyped play environment, this may be something that they have inadvertently achieved; further research would be needed to more substantially explore this particular aspect but some findings of interest emerged. The vignettes have provided examples of boy- or girl-only play activities. Vignettes 1, 2, 4, 6, 9, 10, 13, 15 and 16 were all single gender groups. Interestingly, only one of these was a girls-only group (vignette 6, the group with the lizards) and four of the remaining vignettes were pairs of boys. Four of these vignettes contained larger groups of boys playing together and a further four vignettes (3, 5, 8 and 11) included boys and girls playing together in groups of three or more. There were many other filmed play activities not included in the book. So why are we claiming that this is an environment that does not promote stereotypical play as influenced by cultural expectations? If we are saying that these children bring their culturally shaped identities into the classroom and, alongside this, there is research to show that these identities are gendered by this age (Epstein et al. 2001; McNaughton 2000; Thorne 1993) then how might the provision of open-ended play environments allow engagements between the sexes that avoid gendered expectations of behaviour? We have seen girls being physically active in the company of boys in the vignettes and we have seen boys engaged in extended conversations with other boys and with girls; both of these are commonplace across the filmed material. Nowhere on the many hours of film do we see or hear gendered expectations or statements between peers. In vignette 5, Edward says he will cut the hole in the cardboard box for a door but Sadie replies that she will do it because she is 'stronger'. Edward does not challenge this, and Sadie is in fact taller than Edward. It did seem as though the children had moved beyond gendered expectations to acceptances of equity.

It is also important to state that, early in the filming, Pat began to realise that she was being drawn more regularly to boys' or mixed play activities rather than to girls-only play. The capturing of vignette 6 almost did not happen. Pat was passing and not filming and it was only the raised voice of one of the girls that prompted Pat to begin filming. This relative randomness of the filming undermines the taking of firm conclusions. In addition, Pat did reflect with Andy whether her own status as mother of two boys predisposed her to focus on boys' play.

The occurrence of mixed gender groups chimed with earlier research findings when the 'whatever you want it to be place' was introduced in five reception classes (Broadhead 2004). In watching and deliberating on the filmed play material, Andy and Pat engaged with the notion that open-ended play materials had potential for matching the respective interests arising from the gendered preferences of boys and girls. This may be enough to bring boys and girls together in joint play on a more regular basis and as equals rather than as 'the behaviour police'. The filmed material of mixed gender groups shows significant preoccupations among both boys and girls with joint goal orientation and achievement rather than with a labouring of gendered expectations. There was no general sense across the unit that 'boys do this' and 'girls do this', and that never featured in any of the conversations with the staff either informally or in the semi-structured interviews. The team's perceptions of play interests were expressed in terms of what a child was doing or children were doing together rather than being about what boys or girls might be interested in.

The book has signalled the significance of observing children's play in order to be best positioned to build on expressed interests and pre-occupations. This of itself is by no means a new idea and is certainly expressed as integral within the EYFS. The big challenges in observing children's play for adults are:

- making personal meaning from it in terms of supporting subsequent learning experiences for children, and
- recording it in ways that capture these meanings as progression in learning.

The team at Fishergate were also beset by these challenges. We have seen that that they kept journals of children's activities and achievements which were given to the children when they left the unit. The team moved from direct entries into the journal to keeping observations on dated, sticky parcel labels which then went directly into the book at a later stage, occasionally accompanied by photographs. These were time-consuming activities but did provide opportunities for team members to discuss the children as they were working on the journals and perhaps these reflective conversations were more significant in developing their personal understandings of playful learning and playful pedagogies than the actual business of monitoring individuals.

What this book and others before it have also shown is that, to make meaning from children's play, extended vignettes are needed because the meaningfulness of play is not captured in a few moments or a 'slice' of the action. No early years team would have the time to notate to the extent that these vignettes have. What we do hope the longitudinal nature of this study has shown is that progression in play is most certainly not 'of the moment', and indeed neither is playful learning. Learning and progression are fluid, continuous, incremental and elusive.

As Wood and Bennett (1999:14) point out, pedagogy needs to be informed by theories of learning to be effective in supporting learning. A pedagogical frame that keeps adults constantly busy directing children prevents them from engaging in any mutual bridging of meaning (Stephen 2010: 26) in the way that the team members at Fishergate were able to engage whilst also managing the general busyness of life in an early years unit. However, one rider to this is that we should point out that, as the research finished, the team was shrinking to two members of staff because of pupil numbers at this stage of the year. Andy and Elizabeth, the remaining team members, were aware that this would impact on the previous levels of flexibility that came from a larger team with greater pupil numbers. However, their intention was to retain the outdoor space as it was and the open-ended indoor activities currently in place and to review their roles and responsibilities as the new term progressed; these too would be subject to fluid decision-making.

The book has aimed to convey the sense of changing understandings and changing practice over time for all the members of the early years team at Fishergate and to show just a little of the individualised journey that each of them took. They each had different starting points, although Andy's strongly held views on the value of open-ended play were undoubtedly a catalyst for all of them, and his leadership and continuing enthusiasm for the initiative, despite the inherent challenges, has also undoubtedly had a positive impact. Their individual journeys were personal but shared and the book has also shown the extent to which they found time to talk together, especially about what they were observing as children played. These discussions became a key part of sustaining their engagements with their own learning processes as they thought more about what they were seeing actually meant in terms of children's learning and in terms of what they might subsequently do to promote and extend that learning.

These discussions informed their changes to the planning processes and the gradual changes to their assessment and record-keeping processes as they decided that these processes needed to be slimmed down. They came to see how less time recording meant more time observing, and informed observation led to each of them building their personal funds of knowledge about how children turned open-ended play spaces into 'whatever you want them to be' places. From this, they each formed new understandings of ways in which to engage with children in the setting, and importantly about when to leave the children alone to solve the problem or not – always knowing that children could and would come back at a future date to have another go because the opportunities would always be there. The outdoor space may look chaotic to the untrained eye but it had logic, reason, purpose and structure that all of the children came to understand in due course, including those with special educational needs. Chapter 3 included a quote from Vicky, who had spoken of struggling with 'the messiness of it all' in her early days, but she also said later in her interview:

There's a sense of community that is really strong I think, especially for special needs children. The children are relatively understanding of the fact that D. just barges through but they are also very protective of him. If someone's a bit cross with him, the other children are very protective.

She also said of the parents:

I feel that we work really well in trying to build up relationships with the parents and you see them blossoming in the same way as the children. The mums who have been reluctant to talk, keeping on being positive and saying 'hello', making the time and the space and you feel that they're confident to begin conversations.

It may be that the thinking behind the pedagogies that drive the establishing and sustaining of open-ended play environments also become the thinking behind the reflection and interactions that are needed to help those environments become inclusive for all members of the community. Perhaps a developing capacity to juxtapose the necessary pedagogies (the left hand side of the model) with an understanding of the child's perspectives, intentions and meaning-making (the right hand side of the model) becomes the intellectual impetus for holistically conceptualising the environment for all its members, and we should not underestimate how substantial an intellectual exercise this is for early years educators intent on putting children's interests first and, in so doing, actively acknowledging on a daily basis the importance of home.

There were times when children got wet at Fishergate; we have seen throughout the book that access to water played a big part in the children's outdoor lives and there was also a period when quite large groups of children were using water in the sinks in the toilet area of the unit; they had interpreted the right to access water as applying to all spaces to which they had access. This particular instance is a useful one to reflect on at this point because it illustrates some of the inherent challenges in allowing children to have open access to their play environment. Are there any times when boundaries should be drawn? We have shown across the chapters how such a philosophy links with heightened intellectual challenge for children, but team members did talk in their reflections about the time needed to change the clothing, especially of younger children still learning to manage water (all children were asked to bring and leave a change of clothes in school). They also spoke of rare but nonetheless important occasions when parents complained about the state of the children's clothes. After reflections and discussions the team had addressed these particular aspects in the following ways:

- *Playing with water in the sinks in the toilet*: the team decided that this aspect of play would be stopped because the purpose of the toilets was not for play and the children had access to water in many other places in the unit that were designed for play. This was explained to the children and the activities ceased, with occasional reinforcement.

- *Parental complaints*: whenever new children were being admitted to the unit, Andy would meet the parents as a group and explain the philosophy and practices within the unit relating to open access to all resources and including water. He would explain staff responsibilities in helping children to remain comfortable, the need for spare clothing and suggestions that children did not come to the unit 'in their best clothes'. As children became older and more competent at managing their environment, there was seldom any need to change their clothes but, if they chose to, the majority of the older children would sort themselves out without requesting adult assistance. We saw from the comments from parents in Chapter 5 that, overall, parents appreciated the open-ended nature of the play provision. The few complaints from a small number of parents in their child's early days in the unit would be seen not as grounds for substantial changes in practice, but rather as needing some one-to-one conversations and reassurances.

We do not know from this research but it would certainly have been interesting to pursue this aspect to see if the parents whose children attended Fishergate changed their own parenting practices in any way as a result of seeing how wholeheartedly their children engaged with the naturalness and open-endedness of the play provision in Fishergate.

Child-initiated, child-directed; teacher-initiated, teacher directed: what works in playful learning and how can it be managed?

Bodrova and Leung (2007) discuss the ways in which opportunities for playful engagements can prepare children for the more formal requirements of more substantially adult-directed pedagogies that usually follow on from their experiences in playful learning environments. They state that in play, as we have seen from the research reported in this book too, children learn and exercise self-restraint as they develop and apply rules to their play. Bodrova and Leung also discuss the dilemmas faced by early years educators as they feel required to impose formality on young children when playful experiences seem to be more developmentally appropriate. This was discussed in Chapter 1 as a condition that had applied to early years educators in England over several years, beginning with the introduction of the National Curriculum in 1988 and 'backwashing' into early years provision through a range of other, related policy initiatives.

The publication *Learning, Playing and Interacting* (DCSF 2009b) was the first English curriculum policy statement to explicitly address the issue of creating and sustaining a balanced pedagogy in the early years; in many ways a seminal policy document. It was still available on the Department for Education website in May 2011, although it may have been removed since that time. Copies were sent to schools under the previous Labour government. There was much to commend in this practice guidance document and practitioners certainly welcomed an opportunity to begin to get to grips with debates about what it meant to 'balance the curriculum'. It felt to many like a timely discussion, especially given the previous pressures towards an overemphasis on formality in teaching young children. The document highlights (p. 5) four approaches along a continuum, followed by an explanatory statement:

- Unstructured: Play without adult support;
- Child-initiated play: Adult support for an enabling environment, and sensitive interaction;
- Focused learning: Adult-guided, playful experiential activities;
- Highly structured: Adult directed, little or no play

At one end, too little adult support can limit learning. Whilst play without adults can be rich and purposeful, at times it can become chaotic or repetitive activity which is 'hands-on, brains-off'. At the other end of the scale, too much tightly directed activity deprives children of the opportunity to engage actively with learning.

The example that was cited above of children playing with water in the sinks in the toilet area at Fishergate might be classed under *unstructured play*. There was nothing about the design of the area in which the children were playing, or in relation to prior pedagogical interventions by the early years team (e.g. the provision of materials), that might make this a purposive and developmental opportunity for the children. The significant limit on resources and space suggested that this could only ever be a repetitive activity. It was clearly an experience that the children were enjoying but it allows the making of an important point in this book that providing open-ended play spaces, either outdoors or indoors, is by no means about adults abdicating their responsibilities in providing pedagogical structures appropriate to supporting children in making choices and pursuing their own play themes.

There have been many examples of *child-initiated play* at Fishergate in the vignettes that have been presented; indeed this has been the main focus of the book, to show how the pedagogies of open-ended resource provision can support children in developing new understandings and learning how to resolve conflicts, establish and develop friendships, build life skills and express their cultural heritages in ways that are comfortable and familiar for them. These pedagogies include:

- extended periods of time available for playful engagements alone and with peers on a daily basis;
- team planning that builds on the observed interests and preoccupations of children;

- recognition of and respect for the children's emerging and repeated play themes;
- support for mobility in play scenarios as they move indoors and outdoors, sometimes requiring high levels of physical activity;
- sensitive adult interventions that start from the child's agenda and not the adult's agenda;
- a willingness to allow children to transport materials from play site to play site because play themes are often developed through mobility;
- providing spaces large enough for the more complex designs that older children can create with like-minded peers.

This intensive study of child-initiated play at Fishergate has shown that many of the themes and activities with which children engage are not especially unique to individual children. They appear to share many interests in common that arise, for example, from their shared environment; consider for instance the numbers of times that 'rivers' and 'boats' emerged in children's play here in York – and these were just the vignettes captured in film, suggesting that these may be quite common play themes. Ramps, bridges, slides, the design and inhabiting of domestic spaces, the recreation of what children had seen on television or 'for real', links with parental jobs and magic potions, to name but a few, all featured in more than one play vignette of interacting peers. These are the collective cultural experiences of the children represented through their self-initiated play. We have also noted from study of filmed material and from comments by members of the early years team how the weather and the seasons were continually expressed through the self-initiated play in which the children engaged outdoors.

There have been fewer examples of *focussed learning* in the study, although there have been some, including Kat's (the student teacher) work with the children (vignettes 7 and 8), Debbie's design and building of the boat with a group of girls (Chapter 4) and Andy's powder paint activity (vignette 14). It might be recalled that Andy said that one of the big steps forward for them in developing an open-ended play environment was to 'stop doing topics'. The topic-based approach to planning had led to the replacing of adult-led, playful activities with more child-initiated learning experiences but it is clear that there are still times and places for 'playful, experiential activities', initiated by adults but building from observed interests.

We have not discussed in any detail the kinds of activities that Andy or other team members undertook with the reception children when engaged with literacy and numeracy activity. These tended to be *'structured'* rather than 'playful' although, as the daily programme outlined in Chapter 4 shows, they were also relatively brief but regular. Neither have we discussed at any length the playful engagements that children had with self-initiated literacy and numeracy activities as the remainder of their day unfolded, but the identification of the EYFS learning outcomes and early learning goals against the vignettes show that this play environment gives many opportunities for children to playfully incorporate both sets of skills into their self-initiated play.

Looking to the future of play in early years educational settings

Chapter 1 reviewed the development of early years curriculum guidelines. It made brief mention of the Tickell Review (DoE 2011). The Review provides a number of recommendations and seeks to ensure that the EYFS framework is 'strengthened and simplified' (p. 3). Regrettably, the terms 'playful learning' and 'playful pedagogy' seem to have disappeared from the wider debates about the forward movement of play within the EYFS curriculum. The framing of play is now contained within the phrase 'play-based approaches' (p. 54), although the glossary also contains the term 'child-initiated learning' (p. 52). However, this terminology does not seem to inherently convey the sense of forward movement and forward thinking in embracing and seeking to understand the complexities inherent within the terms and debates that were emerging around playful learning and playful pedagogies in the earlier literature, considered above.

There is a statement (p. 35, para. 3.54) that the reception year is an integral part of the preparation 'for the move to year 1', although there is also an acknowledgement that some reception children are only just four years old. This transition-related statement might be taken as an indication of the likely demise of play in the reception class, once again in our play history in England. If we look then at p. 75, we see an early learning goal relating to phonics and this reminds us, as discussed previously, that when educators feel they will be assessed against particular learning outcomes for children (phonics skills) these can dominate the curriculum to the detriment of the provision of extended periods of time for playful learning opportunities.

Unfortunately, and in addition, the learning characteristics (p. 79) which make reference to play are brief and inevitably tokenistic; these are the messages that get missed when other messages are stronger. It is difficult to see how the rationale for revised areas of learning (p. 85 onwards) can address this tokenism unless playful learning and playful pedagogies are more explicitly engaged with as integral to the processes of learning. There is little reference to the cultural frames of reference that underpin learning and development and which, in the right environment, can be a rich dimension within play. However, play has not been lost altogether from the review and we can all be proactive and responsive as the review and subsequent implementation process rolls forward.

Successive chapters in this book have aimed to show how 'diminished' the learning outcomes seem against the richness and complexity of the play depicted in successive vignettes. It also becomes apparent that, in highly cooperative – and therefore often the richest and most intellectually challenging – play experiences, the assigning of 'outcomes' to 'individuals' seems almost nonsensical as it becomes apparent just how each child is benefitting in her or his own way from the collective, collaborative and cooperative aspects of the playful learning experiences, especially of the older, expert players. In addition, as has been explored, much of what is happening in play cannot be measured or even recorded because it is an internalised experience for the child – as of course is most of our learning. This perhaps explains why the early years team at Fishergate began to reduce their recording times for play and to increase their observation time; only by informed watching could they become truly attuned to each child's learning experiences and to identify the collective interests that emerged in the children's cooperative play.

Friendships, and the development of relationships leading to friendships, were a key feature of life in the unit for the children, and aspects of relation-ship-building and friendship development become very evident from repeated viewing of the filmed material. In watching the play, one becomes aware of how much smiling and laughing goes on between familiar peers, in play and in passing. The unit is their social world for much of their day and the smiles and laughter are a manifestation of their pleasure in being there and in being in the company of those who are familiar to them. Although we were not filming adults, the films have also captured images of smiling and laughing adults, shar-ing jokes and pleasant memories with the children as the day moves forward. Of course the filmed material has also captured more serious moments, and some aspects of conflict have been discussed. The unit and the play were not without conflict but in some cases conflict resolution may become the essence of friendship development; it has also been shown that conflict can contain humour, especially for more mature players. A capacity for conflict resolu-tion is an important part of identity development. Educators perhaps need to become more comfortable with the idea that early years settings should be actively promoting opportunities for conflict resolution, and open-ended play environments do seem to accord with such opportunities to be engaged with in naturalistic ways.

The qualitative differences in the friendships between new, younger chil-dren and the relatively well-established friendship groups of the older children, thoroughly familiar with the materials and sites for play, were also evident from repeated viewings. Yet there are also many instances where younger and older children are together in joint activities and where younger children are thoroughly absorbed in watching the play of groups of older children. This watching clearly involves thinking and over time Andy has come to witness and understand how the younger children gradually begin to replicate some of the play experiences they had observed at an earlier point in time. Watching and thinking are key elements both of intellectual and social growth in the unit, for the children and for the adults.

Across the chapters we see many examples of conversations. These may be brief or extended conversations; they serve for a purposeful exchange of information and it seems as if children are exploring the sense of community that pervades in the unit, a sense that everyone will speak to you and that everyone is interested in you.

We hope the book has unpacked some of the complexities that surround playful learning and playful pedagogies and we hope that the debates and research that can inform our understanding of these complexities can continue beyond the revisions to and implementation of the EYFS. In particular, we hope we have made a good case for bringing the 'whatever you want it to be place', on a large or a small scale, into your early years setting, and perhaps even into Years 1 and 2 in the primary school.

References

Adams, S., Alexander, E., Drummond, M. J. and Moyles, J. (2004) *Inside the Foundation Stage: Recreating the Reception Year*, London: Association of Teachers and Lecturers.

Anning, A. (1997) *The First Years at School*, Buckingham: Open University Press.

Anning, A. and Edwards, A. (1999) *Promoting Children's Learning from Birth to Five: Developing the new early years professional*, Buckingham: Open University Press.

Armistead, J. (2010) 'Reflecting on ethical considerations around young children's engagement when researching children's perspectives', in A. Campbell and P. Broadhead (eds) *Working with Children and Young People: Ethical debates and practices across disciplines and continents*, Bern: Peter Lang.

Arnold, C. (2003) *Observing Harry*, Maidenhead: Open University Press.

Aubrey, C. (2004) 'Implementing the Foundation Stage in Reception Classes', *British Educational Research Journal* 30 (5): 633–56.

Aureli, F. and de Waal, F. B. M. (2000) *Natural Conflict Resolution*, Berkeley: University of California Press.

Bennett, N. and Kell, J. (1989) *A Good Start? Four Year Olds in School*, Oxford: Blackwell.

Bennett, N., Wood, E. and Rogers, S. (1997) *Teaching through Play: Teachers' thinking and classroom practice*, Buckingham: Open University Press.

Bodrova, E. (2008) 'Make-believe play versus academic skills: a Vygotskyan approach to today's dilemmas of early childhood education', *European Early Childhood Education Research Journal* 16 (3): 357–69.

Bodrova, E. and Leung, D. J. (2007) 'Playing for academic skills', *Children in Europe*, Vygotsky Issue: 10–11.

Broadhead, P. (2004) *Early Years Play and Learning: Developing social skills and cooperation*, London: RoutledgeFalmer.

Broadhead, P. (2006) 'Developing an understanding of young children's learning through play: the place of observation, interaction and reflection', *British Educational Research Journal* 32 (2): 191–207.

Broadhead, P. (2009) 'Conflict resolution and children's behaviour: observing and understanding social and cooperative play in early years educational settings', *Early Years* 29 (2): 105–18.

Broadhead, P. (2010) 'Building friendships through playful learning in the early years', in J. Moyles (ed.) *The Excellence of Play*, Maidenhead: Open University Press.

Broadhead, P., Howard, J. and Wood, E. (2010) *Play and Learning in the Early Years*, London: Sage.

Brock, A. (ed.) (1999) *Into the Enchanted Forest*, Stoke-on-Trent: Trentham Books.

Brooker, L. (2002) *Starting School: Young Children Learning Cultures*, Buckingham: Open University Press.

Brooker, L. (2008) *Supporting Transition in the Early Years*, Maidenhead: Open University Press.

Brooker, L. (2010) 'Learning to play in a cultural context', in P. Broadhead, J. Howard and E. Wood (eds) *Play and Learning in the Early Years: From research to practice*, London: Sage.

Brooker, L., Rogers, S., Ellis, D., Hallett, E. and Roberts-Holmes, G. (2010) Practitioners' Experiences of the Early Years Foundation Stage, *Research Brief DFE-RB029*, August.

Brown, F. (2003) 'Compound flexibility: the role of playwork in child development', in F. Brown (ed.) *Playwork: Theory and practice*, Buckingham: Open University Press.

Bruce, T. (1987) *Early Childhood Education*, London: Hodder Arnold.

Butovskaya, M., Veerbeek, P., Ljunberg, T. and Lunardini, A. (2000) 'A multicultural view of peacemaking among young children', in F. Aureli and F. B. M. de Waal (eds) *Natural Conflict Resolution*, Berkeley: University of California Press.

CACE (Central Advisory Council for England) (1967) *Children and Their Primary Schools*. The Plowden Report, London: HMSO.

Carr, M., Jones, C. and Lee, W. (2005) 'Beyond listening: can assessment practice play a part?', in A. Clark, A.-T. Kjorholt and P. Moss (eds) *Beyond Listening: Children's perspectives on early childhood services*, Bristol: Policy Press.

Clark, A. (2010) *Transforming Children's Spaces: Children's and adults participation in designing learning environments*, London: Routledge.

Clark, A. and Moss, P. (2001) *Listening to Young Children: The mosaic approach*, London: National Children's Bureau.

Claxton, G. (1995) 'What kind of learning does self-assessment drive?', *Assessment in Education* 2 (3): 339–43.

Cleave, S. and Brown, S. (1991) *Early to School: Four year olds in infant classes*, Windsor: NFER-Nelson.

Connolly, P (2004) *Boys and Schooling in the Early Years*, London: RoutledgeFalmer.

Cosaro, W. A. (1997) *The Sociology of Childhood*, London: Sage Publications.

Cosaro, W. A. and Molinari, L. (2001) 'Entering and observing in children's worlds: a reflection on a longitudinal ethnography of early education in Italy', in P. Christensen and A. James (eds) *Research with Children: Perspectives and practices*, London: Routledge/Falmer.

Costa, A. L. (1991) 'The search for intelligent life', in A. L. Costa (ed.) *Developing Minds: A resource book for teaching thinking, Vol. 1* (revised edition), Alexandria, VA: Association for Supervision and Curriculum Development.

Cox, C. B. and Dyson, A. E. (eds) (1971) *The Black Papers on Education*, London: Davis-Poynter.

Dahlberg, G. and Moss, P. (2005) *Ethics and Politics in Early Childhood Education*, London: Routledge.

David, T., Goouch, K. and Powell, S. (2010) 'Play and prescription: the impact of national developments in England', in M. Kernan and E. Singer (eds) *Peer Relationships in Early Childhood Education and Care*, London: Routledge.

DCSF (Department for Children, Schools and Families) (2009a) *Independent Review of the Primary Curriculum: Final Report*. The Rose Review, Nottingham: DCSF Publications.

DCSF (2009b) *Learning, Playing and Interacting*, London: QCA.

DCSF (2009c) *Early Years Learning and Development: Literature Review*, London: DCSF.

DfES (Department for Education and Skills) (2007) *The Early Years Foundation Stage*, London: DfES.

DoE (Department of Education) (2011) *The Early Years: Foundations for life, health and learning*. A Report by Dame Clare Tickell, London: DoE.

Education and Skills Committee (2005) *Education outside the Classroom*. Second Report of Session 2004–05. Report, Together with Formal Minutes, Oral and Written Evidence (HC 120), London: The Stationery Office.

Edwards, S. (2006) ' "Stop talking about culture as geography": early childhood teachers' conceptions of sociocultural theory as an informant to curriculum', *Contemporary Issues in Early Childhood* 7 (3): 238–52.

Edwards, S. (2009) *Early Childhood Education and Care: A sociocultural approach*, Castle Hill, NSW: Pademelon Press.

Elkonin, D. B. (2005) 'The psychology of play: preface', *Journal of Russian and East European Psychology* 43 (1): 11–21 (original work published 1978).

Epstein, D., Kehily, M. and Redman, P. (2001) 'Boys and girls come out to play: making masculinities and femininities in school playgrounds', *Men and Masculinities* 4 (2): 158–72.

Erikson, E. H. (1969) *Childhood and Society* (2nd edition), New York: Norton.

Factor, J. (2009) ' "It's only play if you get to choose": children's perspective of play and adult's interventions', in C. D. Clark (ed.) *Transactions at Play; Play and Culture Studies, Vol. 9*, New York: University Press of America.

Fleer, M. (2002) 'Socio-cultural theory: rebuilding the theoretical foundations of early childhood education', *Early Education: Policy Curriculum and Discourse* 54 (1): 105–21.

Fleer, M. and Richardson, C. (2004) *Observing and Planning in Early Childhood Settings: Using a sociocultural approach*, Canberra: Early Childhood Australia.

Fongay, P. (2001) *Psychoanalysis and Attachment Theory*, London: Karnac.

Fongay, P., Steele, H., Higgert, A. and Target, M. (1994) 'The theory and practice of resilience', *Journal of Child Psychology and Psychiatry* 35 (2): 231–57.

Fry, D. P. (2000) 'Conflict management in cross-cultural perspective', in F. Aureli, and F. B. M. de Waal (eds) *Natural Conflict Resolution*, Berkeley: University of California Press.

Furedi, F. (2002) *Culture of Fear: Risk-Taking and the Morality of Low Expectations*, London: Continuum.

Gergen, M. M. and Gergen, K. J. (2003) 'Qualitative inquiry: tensions and transformations', in N. K. Denzin and Y. S. Lincoln (eds) *The Landscape of Qualitative Research: Theories and issues*, London: Sage Publications.

Gill, T. (2006) 'Home zones in the UK: history, policy and the impact on youth', *Children, Youth and Environments* 16: 90–103.

Gleave, J. (2010) *Making It Our Place: Community views on children's play*, London: National Children's Bureau.

Greenfield, S. (2000) *The Private Life of the Brain*, St Ives: Penguin.

Hedegaard, M. (2008) 'A cultural-historical theory of children's development', in M. Hedegaard, and M. Fleer, *Studying Children: A cultural historical approach*, Berkshire: Open University Press.

Henricks, T. S. (2010) 'Play as ascending meaning revisited: for types of assertive play', in E. E. Nwokah (ed.) *Play as Engagement and Communication: Play and Culture Studies Vol. 10*, Lanham, MD: University Press of America.

Howard, J. (2010) 'Making the most of play in the early years: the importance of children's perceptions', in P. Broadhead, J. Howard and E. Wood (eds) *Play and Learning in the Early Years: From research to practice*, London: Sage.

Jarvis, P. (2010) '"Born to play": the biocultural roots of rough and tumble play, and its impact on young children's learning and development', in P. Broadhead, J. Howard and E. Wood (eds) *Play and Learning in the Early Years: From research to practice*, London: Sage.

Little, H. and Wyver, S. (2010) 'Individual differences in children's risk perception and appraisals in outdoor play environments', *International Journal of Early Years Education* 18 (4): 297–313.

Marsh, J. (1999) 'Batman and Batwoman go to school: popular culture in the literacy curriculum', *International Journal of Early Years Education* 7 (2): 117–31.

Marsh, J. (2000) 'But I want to fly too: girls and superhero play in the infant classroom', *Gender and Education* 12 (2): 209–20.

Martlew, J., Stephen, C. and Ellis, J. (2011) 'Play in the primary school classroom? The experience of teachers supporting children's learning through a new pedagogy', *Early Years*, 31 (1): 71–83.

Maynard, T. and Chicken, S. (2010) 'Through a different lens: exploring Reggio Emilia in a Welsh context', *Early Years* 30 (1): 29–39.

McNaughton, G. (2000) *Rethinking Gender in Early Childhood Education*, London: Paul Chapman.

Moss, P. and Petrie, P. (2002) *From Children's Services to Children's Spaces: Public policy, children and childhood*, London: Routledge.

Moyles, J. (1989) *Just Playing? The role and status of play in early childhood education*, Buckingham: Open University Press.

Moyles, J. (ed.) (2010) *Thinking about Play: Developing a reflective approach*, Maidenhead: Open University Press.

Nicholson, S. (1971) 'How not to cheat children: the theory of loose parts', *Landscape Architecture* 62: 30–5.

Nutbrown, C. (2006) *Threads of Thinking: Young children learning and the role of early education* (3rd edition), London: Sage.

O'Dea, J. and Erikson, M. (eds) (2010) *Childhood Obesity Prevention: International research, controversy and interventions*, Oxford: Oxford University Press.

Ofsted (Office for Standards in Education) (2004) *Outdoor Education: Aspects of good practice*, HMI 2151.

Pramling-Samuelsson, I. and Fleer, M. (eds) (2009) *Play and Learning in Early Childhood Settings*, New York: Springer Publishing Company.

QCA (Qualifications and Curriculum Authority) (2000) *Curriculum Guidance for the Foundation Stage*, London: QCA Publications.

QCA (2003) *Foundation Stage Profile*, London: DfES.

QCA (2008) *The Early Years Foundation Stage Profile Handbook*, London: DCSF.

Ramsden, E. and Jones, P. (2010) 'Children as active agents in gaining and giving assent: involving children as co-researchers', in A. Campbell and P. Broadhead (eds) *Working with Children and Young People: Ethical debates and practices across disciplines and continents*, Bern: Peter Lang.

Reynolds, G. and Jones, E. (1997) *Master Players: Learning from children at play*, New York: Teachers College Press.

Roberts, H. (2001) 'Listening to children: and hearing them', in P. Christensen and A. James (eds) *Research with Children: Perspectives and practices*, London: RoutledgeFalmer.

Robson, S. (2010) 'Self-regulation and metacognition in young children's self-initiated play and Reflective Dialogue', *International Journal of Early Years Education* 18 (3): 227–41.

Rogers, S. and Evans, J. (2008) *Inside Role-Play in Early Childhood Education*, London: Routledge.

Rogoff, B. (1990) *Apprenticeships in Thinking: Cognitive development in social context*, New York: Oxford University Press.

Rogoff, B. (1994) 'Developing understanding of the idea of communities of learners', *Mind, Culture and Activity* 4 (1): 75–91.

Rogoff, B. (2003) *The Cultural Nature of Human Development*, Oxford: Oxford University Press.

Scott, D. and Morrison, M. (2006) *Key Ideas in Educational Research*, London: Continuum.

Statutory Framework for the Early Years Foundation Stage (2007) London: DfES.

Stephen, C. (2010) 'Pedagogy: the silent partner in early years learning', *Early Years* 30 (1): 15–28.

Stephenson, A. (2003) 'Physical risk-taking: dangerous or endangered?', *Early Years* 23 (1): 35–43.

Sylva, K., Melhuish, E., Sammons, P., Siraj-Blatchford, I. and Taggart, B. (2010) *Early Childhood Matters: Evidence from the Effective Pre-school and Primary Education Project (EPPE)*, London: Routledge.

Taylor, C. (2008) 'Playwork and the theory of loose parts', in F. Brown and C. Taylor (eds) *Foundations of Playwork*, Maidenhead: Open University Press.

Tishman, S., Jay, E. and Perkins, D. N. (1993) 'Teaching thinking dispositions: from transmission to enculturation', *Theory into Practice* 32 (Summer): 147–53.

Thorne, B. (1993) *Gender Play: Boys and girls in school*, Buckingham: Open University Press.

Tovey, H. (2007) *Playing Outdoors: Spaces and places, risks and challenges*, Maidenhead: Open University Press.

Vandenbroeck, M. (1999) *The View of the Yeti*, The Hague: Bernard van Leer Foundation.

Van Oers, B. (2005) 'The potentials of imagination', *Inquiry: Critical Thinking across the Disciplines* 24 (4): 5–17.

Verbeek P., Hartup, W. W. and Collins, W. A. (2000) 'Conflict management in children and adolescents', in F. Aureli and F. B. M. de Waal (eds) *Natural Conflict Resolution*, Berkeley: University of California Press.

Vygotsky, L. (1966) 'Play and its role in the mental development of the child', *Vosprosy psikhologii* 12 (6): 62–76.

Vygotsky, L. (1986) *Thought and Language*, Cambridge, MA: MIT Press.

Webster, L. and Broadhead, P. (2010) 'Their life, their choice: ethical challenges for supporting children and young people in the self-management of Type 1 diabetes', in A. Campbell and P. Broadhead (eds) *Working with Children and Young People: Ethical debates and practices across disciplines and continents* Bern: Peter Lang.

Weedon, C. (2004) *Identity and Culture: Narratives of Difference and Belonging*, Buckingham: Open University Press.

Weeks, J. (1990) 'The value of difference', in J. Rutherford (ed.) *Identity, Community Culture, Difference*, London: Lawrence and Wishart.

Whitebread, D. (ed.) (2002) *Teaching and Learning in the Early Years*, London: RoutledgeFalmer.

Whitebread, D., Bingham, S., Grau, V., Pino Pasternak, D. and Sangster, C. (2007) 'The development of metacognition and self-regulated learning in young children: the role of collaborative and peer-assisted learning', *Journal of Cognitive Education and Psychology* 6 (3): 433–55.

Wood, E. (1997) 'New directions in play: consensus or collision', *Education 3–13* 35 (4): 309–20.

Wood, E. and Attfield, J. (2005) *Play, Learning and the Early Childhood Curriculum*, London: Paul Chapman.

Wood, E. and Bennett, N. (1999) 'Progression and continuity in early childhood education: tensions and contradictions', *International Journal of Early Years Education* 7 (1): 5–16.

Worthington, M. (2010a) 'Play is a complex landscape: imagination and symbolic meanings', in P. Broadhead, J. Howard and E. Wood (eds) *Play and Learning in the Early Years: From research to practice*, London: Sage.

Worthington, M. (2010b) 'This is a different calculator with computer games on: reflecting on children's symbolic play in the digital age', in J. Moyles (ed.) *Thinking about Play: Developing a reflective approach*, Maidenhead: Open University Press.

Index